TO:

_____

The LORD bless thee, and keep thee.

Numbers 6:24

FROM:

_____

Daily Inspiration for Women of Color
Copyright 2001 by Zondervan
ISBN 0-310-80091-9

All Scripture quotations are taken from the *King
James Version* of the Bible.

Requests for information should be addressed to:
Inspirio, The gift group of Zondervan
Grand Rapids, Michigan 49530
http://www.inspiriogifts.com

Associate Editor: Molly C. Detweiler
Assistant Editor: Heidi A. Carvella
Design Manager: Amy E. Langeler
Cover Design: David Carlson
Interior Design: Laura Blost

Printed in the United States of America
02 03 04/OP/ 4 3

DAILY
INSPIRATION
FOR
WOMEN of COLOR

Compiled by
Snapdragon Editorial Group, Inc.

inspirio™

TABLE OF CONTENTS

Abundance 12

Acceptance 14

Aging 16

Anger 18

Answered Prayer 20

Anxiety 22

Assurance 24

Atonement 27

Beauty 31

Bible Study 33

Blessing 35

Blood of Jesus 37

Boldness 40

Celebration 42

Challenge 44

Children 46

Comfort 48

Commitment 52

Communication 54

Compassion 56

Confidence 60

Confusion 64

Contentment 66

Courage 68

Despair 71

Disappointment 73

Discernment 75

Discipleship 77

Discipline 79

Encouragement 81

Evangelism 83

Everlasting Life 85

Faith 87

Faithfulness 89

Family 91

Fellowship 93

Finances 95

Forgiveness 97

Freedom 100

Friendship 102

Giving 104

God's Presence 106

God's Word 109

Grace III

Grief 115

Guidance 117

Guilt 121

Happiness 123

Health and Healing 126

Heaven 128

Holiness 130

Holy Spirit 133

Honesty 137

Hope 139

Hospitality 141

Humility 143

Integrity 145

Intercession 148

Joy 150

Justice 152

Kindness 156

Kingdom of God 158

Leadership 161

Life 162

Loneliness 166

Love 170

Meditation 175

Mercy 177

Ministry 179

Money 182

Obedience 185

Pain 187

Parenting 189

Patience 191

Peace 193

Perseverance 197

Power 199

Praise 203

Prayer 207

Pride 210

Priorities 212

Prophecy 214

Protection 216

Provision 220

Purity 224

Purpose 227

Reconciliation 229

Relationships 231

Repentance 233

Rest 235

Restoration 237

Revival 239

Reward 241

Righteousness 243

Sacrifice 247

Salvation 250

Security 254

Self-control 256

Self-esteem 258

Speech 260

Stewardship 262

Strength 263

Struggle 265

Success 268

Suffering 272

Talents and Gifts 276

Temptation 278

Thankfulness 280

Time 284

Tithes and Offerings . .286

Trouble 288

Trust 293

Truth 298

Unity 302

Victory 304

Wisdom 306

Work 310

Worry 314

Worship 316

INTRODUCTION

The Word of God tells us in 2 Timothy 3:16: All scripture is given by inspiration of God, and is profitable for doctrine, for reproof, for correction, for instruction in righteousness: that the man of God may be perfect, thoroughly furnished unto all good works. That scripture is perhaps the most beautiful of all, because it assures us that God's words are timeless. They apply just as certainly, just as powerfully to our lives today as they did on the day they were first recorded.

As you open these pages, it is our prayer that your heart will be quickened by the Spirit of God, and you will be encouraged to trust God with every concern you have—no matter how great or small. God bless you on your way!

ABUNDANCE

Said Jesus, "I am come that they might have life, and that they might have it more abundantly."

John 10:10

How excellent is thy lovingkindness, O God! Therefore the children of men put their trust under the shadow of thy wings. They shall be abundantly satisfied with the fatness of thy house; and thou shalt make them drink of the river of thy pleasures.

Psalm 36:7–8

Ye know the grace of our Lord Jesus Christ, that, though he was rich, yet for your sakes he became poor, that ye through his poverty might be rich.

2 Corinthians 8:9

"My people shall be satisfied with my goodness," saith the LORD.

Jeremiah 31:14

The grace of our Lord was exceeding
abundant with faith and love which is in
Christ Jesus.

1 Timothy 1:14

Unto God that is able to do exceeding
abundantly above all that we ask or think,
according to the power that worketh in us,
Unto him be glory in the church by Christ
Jesus throughout all ages, world without end.
Amen.

Ephesians 3:20–21

The meek shall inherit the earth; and shall
delight themselves in the abundance of
peace.

Psalm 37:11

Jesus said, "Whosoever hath, to him shall be
given, and he shall have more abundance."

Matthew 13:12

ACCEPTANCE

Blessed be the God and Father of our Lord
Jesus Christ, who hath blessed us with all
spiritual blessings in heavenly places in Christ:
According as he hath chosen us in him before
the foundation of the world, that we should
be holy and without blame before him in love:
Having predestinated us unto the adoption of
children by Jesus Christ to himself, according
to the good pleasure of his will, To the praise
of the glory of his grace, wherein he hath
made us accepted in the beloved.

Ephesians 1:3–6

The God of patience and consolation grant
you to be likeminded one toward another
according to Christ Jesus: That ye may with
one mind and one mouth glorify God, even
the Father of our Lord Jesus Christ.
Wherefore receive ye one another, as Christ
also received us to the glory of God.

Romans 15:5–7

The LORD taketh pleasure in those who fear Him, in those who hope in his mercy.

Psalm 147:11

I am continually with thee, LORD: thou hast holden me by my right hand. Thou shalt guide me with thy counsel, and afterward receive me to glory. Whom have I in heaven but thee? and there is none upon earth that I desire beside thee.

Psalm 73:23–25

Jesus said, "Let not your heart be troubled: ye believe in God, believe also in me. In my Father's house are many mansions: if it were not so, I would have told you. I go to prepare a place for you. And if I go and prepare a place for you, I will come again, and receive you unto myself; that where I am, there ye may be also."

John 14:1–3

AGING

By [wisdom] thy days shall be multiplied, and the years of thy life shall be increased.

Proverbs 9:11

Forget not my law; but let thine heart keep my commandments: For length of days, and long life, and peace, shall they add to thee.

Proverbs 3:1–2

"Even to your old age I am he; and even to hoar hairs will I carry you: I have made, and I will bear; even I will carry, and will deliver you," saith the Lord.

Isaiah 46:4

The hoary head is a crown of glory, if it be found in the way of righteousness.

Proverbs 16:31

The glory of young men is their strength; and the beauty of old men is the gray head.

Proverbs 20:29

The fear of the LORD prolongeth days.

Proverbs 10:27

The righteous shall flourish like the palm
tree: he shall grow like a cedar in Lebanon.
Those that be planted in the house of the
LORD shall flourish in the courts of our God.
They shall still bring forth fruit in old age;
they shall be fat and flourishing.

Psalm 92:12—14

The LORD shall bless thee out of Zion: and
thou shalt see the good of Jerusalem all the
days of thy life. Yea, thou shalt see thy
children's children, and peace upon Israel.

Psalm 128:5—6

LORD, thou hast been our dwelling place in
all generations. Before the mountains were
brought forth, or ever thou hadst formed the
earth and the world, even from everlasting to
everlasting, thou art God.

Psalm 90:1—2

ANGER

He that is slow to anger is better than the mighty; and he that ruleth his spirit than he that taketh a city.

Proverbs 16:32

He that is slow to wrath is of great understanding: but he that is hasty of spirit exalteth folly.

Proverbs 14:29

My beloved brethren; let every man be swift to hear, slow to speak, slow to wrath: For the wrath of men worketh not the righteousness of God.

James 1:19—20

The LORD is merciful and gracious, slow to anger, and plenteous in mercy. He will not always chide: neither will he keep his anger for ever.

Psalm 103:8—9

A wrathful man stirreth up strife: but he that is slow to anger appeaseth strife.

Proverbs 15:18

A soft answer turneth away wrath: but grievous words stir up anger.

Proverbs 15:1

Who is a God like unto thee, that pardoneth iniquity, and passeth by the transgression of the remnant of his heritage? he retaineth not his anger for ever, because he delighteth in mercy. He will turn again, he will have compassion upon us; he will subdue our iniquities; and thou wilt cast all their sins into the depths of the sea.

Micah 7:18—19

The discretion of a man deferreth his anger; and it is his glory to pass over a transgression.

Proverbs 19:11

ANSWERED PRAYER

Jesus said, "Ask, and it shall be given you; seek, and ye shall find; knock, and it shall be opened unto you: For every one that asketh receiveth; and he that seeketh findeth; and to him that knocketh it shall be opened."

Matthew 7:7–8

This is the confidence that we have in God, that, if we ask any thing according to his will, he heareth us: And if we know that he hear us, whatsoever we ask, we know that we have the petitions that we desired of him.

1 John 5:14–15

Jesus said, "Whatsoever ye shall ask in my name, that will I do, that the Father may be glorified in the Son. If ye shall ask any thing in my name, I will do it."

John 14:13–14

God will regard the prayer of the destitute, and not despise their prayer.

Psalm 102:17

"It shall come to pass, that before they call, I will answer; and while they are yet speaking, I will hear," saith the Lord.

Isaiah 65:24

"Because he hath set his love upon me, therefore will I deliver him: I will set him on high, because he hath known my name. He shall call upon me, and I will answer him: I will be with him in trouble; I will deliver him, and honour him," saith the Lord.

Psalm 91:14–15

Jesus said, "Whatsoever ye shall ask the Father in my name, he will give it you."

John 16:23

The LORD has heard the voice of my weeping. The LORD hath heard my supplication; the LORD will receive my prayer.

Psalm 6:8–9

●

ANXIETY

I sought the LORD, and he heard me, and
delivered me from all my fears.

Psalm 34:4

Be careful for nothing; but in every thing by
prayer and supplication with thanksgiving let
your requests be made known unto God.
And the peace of God, which passeth all
understanding, shall keep your hearts and
minds through Christ Jesus.

Philippians 4:6–7

My flesh and my heart faileth: but God is
the strength of my heart, and my portion
for ever.

Psalm 73:26

Jesus said, "In the world ye shall have
tribulation: but be of good cheer; I have
overcome the world."

John 16:33

I the LORD thy God will hold thy right hand,
saying unto thee; Fear not; I will help thee.

Isaiah 41:13

Fear was on every side ... But I trusted in
thee, O LORD: I said, Thou art my God.

Psalm 31:13–14

Humble yourselves ... under the mighty hand
of God, that he may exalt you in due time:
Casting all your care upon him; for he careth
for you.

1 Peter 5:6–7

In God I will praise his word, in God I have
put my trust; I will not fear what flesh can do
unto me.

Psalm 56:4

Be still, and know that I am God.

Psalm 46:10

ASSURANCE

I know whom I have believed, and am persuaded that God is able to keep that which I have committed unto him against that day.

2 Timothy 1:12

Jesus said, "My sheep hear my voice, and I know them, and they follow me: And I give unto them eternal life; and they shall never perish, neither shall any man pluck them out of my hand. My Father, which gave them me, is greater than all; and no man is able to pluck them out of my Father's hand."

John 10:27–29

God hath appointed a day, in the which he will judge the world in righteousness by that man [Jesus Christ] whom he hath ordained; whereof he hath given assurance unto all men, in that he hath raised him from the dead.

Acts 17:31

Who shall separate us from the love of
Christ? Shall tribulation, or distress, or
persecution, or famine, or nakedness, or peril,
or sword? ... Nay, in all these things we are
more than conquerors through him that
loved us. For I am persuaded, that neither
death, nor life, nor angels, nor principalities,
nor powers, nor things present, nor things to
come, Nor height, nor depth, nor any other
creature, shall be able to separate us from
the love of God, which is in Christ Jesus
our Lord.

Romans 8:35, 37–39

The mountains shall depart, and the hills be
removed; but my kindness shall not depart
from thee, neither shall the covenant of my
peace be removed, saith the LORD that hath
mercy on thee.

Isaiah 54:10

As far as the east is from the west, so far hath
God removed our transgressions from us.

Psalm 103:12

I the LORD thy God will hold thy right hand,
saying unto thee, Fear not; I will help thee.

Isaiah 41:13

The work of righteousness shall be peace;
and the effect of righteousness quietness and
assurance for ever.

Isaiah 32:17

ATONEMENT

Herein is love, not that we loved God, but that he loved us, and sent his son to be the propitiation for our sins.

1 John 4:10

For all have sinned, and come short of the glory of God; Being justified freely by his grace through the redemption that is in Christ Jesus: Whom God hath set forth to be a propitiation through faith in his blood, to declare his righteousness for the remission of sins that are past, through the forbearance of God; To declare, I say, at this time his righteousness: that he might be just, and the justifier of him which believeth in Jesus.

Romans 3:23–26

God commendeth his love toward us, in that, while we were yet sinners, Christ died for us. Much more then, being now justified by his blood, we shall be saved from wrath through him.

Romans 5:8–9

Christ was once offered to bear the sins of
many; and unto them that look for him shall
he appear the second time without sin
unto salvation.

Hebrews 9:28

As they were eating, Jesus took bread, and
blessed it, and brake it, and gave it to the
disciples, and said, Take, eat; this is my body.
And he took the cup, and gave thanks, and
gave it to them, saying, Drink ye all of it;
This is my blood of the new testament,
which is shed for many for the remission
of sins.

Matthew 26:26—28

God hath made Christ to be sin for us, who
knew no sin; that we might be made the
righteousness of God in him.

2 Corinthians 5:21

Hereunto were ye called: because Christ also suffered for us, leaving us an example, that ye should follow his steps. ... Who his own self bare our sins in his own body on the tree, that we, being dead to sins, should live unto righteousness: by whose stripes ye were healed. For ye were as sheep going astray; but are now returned unto the Shepherd and Bishop of your souls.

1 Peter 2:21, 24—25

If any man sin, we have an advocate with the Father, Jesus Christ the righteous: And he is the propitiation for our sins: and not for ours only, but also for the sins of the whole world.

1 John 2:1—2

Ye know that ye were not redeemed with corruptible things, as silver and gold, from your vain conversation received by tradition from your fathers; But with the precious blood of Christ, as of a lamb without blemish and without spot.

1 Peter 1:18—19

If the blood of bulls and of goats, and the
ashes of an heifer sprinkling the unclean,
sanctifieth to the purifying of the flesh: how
much more shall the blood of Christ, who
through the eternal Spirit offered himself
without spot to God, purge your conscience
from dead works to serve the living God?

Hebrews 9:13–14

In Christ Jesus ye who sometimes were far
off are made nigh by the blood of Christ. For
he is our peace, who hath made both one,
and hath broken down the middle wall of
partition between us.

Ephesians 2:13–14

You, being dead in your sins and the
uncircumcision of your flesh, hath he
quickened together with him, having forgiven
you all trespasses; Blotting out the
handwriting of ordinances that was against
us, which was contrary to us, and took it out
of the way, nailing it to his cross.

Colossians 2:13–14

BEAUTY

Favour is deceitful, and beauty is vain: but a woman that feareth the LORD, she shall be praised. Give her of the fruit of her hands; and let her own works praise her in the gates.

Proverbs 31:30–31

The LORD seeth not as man seeth; for man looketh on the outward appearance, but the LORD looketh on the heart.

1 Samuel 16:7

How beautiful upon the mountains are the feet of him that bringeth good tidings, that publisheth peace; that bringeth good tidings of good, that publisheth salvation; that said unto Zion, Thy God reigneth!

Isaiah 52:7

One thing have I desired of the LORD, that will I seek after; that I may dwell in the house of the LORD all the days of my life, to behold the beauty of the LORD, and to inquire in his temple.

Psalm 27:4

How great is God's goodness, and how great
is his beauty!

Zechariah 9:17

The LORD taketh pleasure in his people: he
will beautify the meek with salvation. Let the
saints be joyful in glory: let them sing aloud
upon their beds.

Psalm 149:4–5

God has made every thing beautiful in
his time.

Ecclesiastes 3:11

BIBLE STUDY

Whoso looketh into the perfect law of
liberty, and continueth therein, he being not
a forgetful hearer, but a doer of the work, this
man shall be blessed in his deed.

James 1:25

Thy word have I hid in mine heart, that I
might not sin against thee, O Lord.

Psalm 119:11

Thy testimonies are wonderful, O Lord:
therefore doth my soul keep them. The
entrance of thy words giveth light; it giveth
understanding unto the simple.

Psalm 119:129—130

Let the word of Christ dwell in you richly in
all wisdom; teaching and admonishing one
another in psalms and hymns and spiritual
songs, singing with grace in your hearts to
the Lord.

Colossians 3:16

Thy words were found, and I did eat them; and thy word was unto me the joy and rejoicing of mine heart: for I am called by thy name, O LORD God of hosts.

Jeremiah 15:16

Study to show thyself approved unto God, a workman that needeth not to be ashamed, rightly dividing the word of truth.

2 Timothy 2:15

Thy hands have made me and fashioned me, Lord: give me understanding, that I may learn thy commandments.

Psalm 119:73

BLESSING

Blessed be the God and Father of our Lord
Jesus Christ, who hath blessed us with all
spiritual blessings in heavenly places in
Christ.

Ephesians 1:3

Jesus said, "Blessed are the poor in spirit: for
theirs is the kingdom of heaven. Blessed are
they that mourn: for they shall be comforted.
Blessed are the meek: for they shall inherit
the earth. Blessed are they which do hunger
and thirst after righteousness: for they shall
be filled. Blessed are the merciful: for they
shall obtain mercy. Blessed are the pure in
heart: for they shall see God. Blessed are the
peacemakers: for they shall be called the
children of God. Blessed are they which are
persecuted for righteousness' sake: for theirs
is the kingdom of heaven."

Matthew 5:3–10

We know that all things work together for
good to them that love God, to them who are
the called according to his purpose.

Romans 8:28

Blessed be he that cometh in the name of
the LORD.

Psalm 118:26

The LORD will give strength unto his people;
the LORD will bless his people with peace.

Psalm 29:11

Thou, LORD, will bless the righteous;
with favour wilt thou compass him as with
a shield.

Psalm 5:12

BLOOD OF JESUS

Jesus took the cup, and gave thanks, and gave it to [his disciples], saying, Drink ye all of it; For this is my blood of the new testament, which is shed for many for the remission of sins.

Matthew 26:27–28

It pleased the Father that in Christ should all fulness dwell; And, having made peace through the blood of his cross, by him to reconcile all things unto himself; by him, I say, whether they be things in earth, or things in heaven. And you, that were sometime alienated and enemies in your mind by wicked works, yet now hath he reconciled in the body of his flesh through death, to present you holy and unblameable and unreproveable in his sight.

Colossians 1:19–22

God commendeth his love toward us, in that, while we were yet sinners, Christ died for us. Much more then, being now justified by his blood, we shall be saved from wrath through him.

Romans 5:9

Ye know that ye were not redeemed with corruptible things, as silver and gold, from your vain conversation received by tradition from your fathers; But with the precious blood of Christ, as of a lamb without blemish and without spot. ... Who by him do believe in God, that raised him up from the dead, and gave him glory; that your faith and hope might be in God.

1 Peter 1:18–19, 21

Grace be unto you ... from Jesus Christ, who is the faithful witness, and the first begotten of the dead, and the prince of the kings of the earth. Unto him that loved us, and washed us from our sins in his own blood, and hath made us kings and priests unto God and his Father; to him be glory and dominion for ever and ever. Amen.

Revelation 1:4–6

Now in Christ Jesus ye who sometimes were far off are made nigh by the blood of Christ. For he is our peace, who hath made both one, and hath broken down the middle wall of partition between us; Having abolished in his flesh the enmity, even the law of commandments contained in ordinances; for to make in himself of twain one new man, so making peace; And that he might reconcile both unto God in one body by the cross, having slain the enmity thereby: And came and preached peace to you which were afar off, and to them that were nigh. For through him we both have access by one Spirit unto the Father. Now therefore ye are no more strangers and foreigners, but fellowcitizens with the saints, and of the household of God.

Ephesians 2:13–19

BOLDNESS

Seeing then that we have a great high priest, that is passed into the heavens, Jesus the Son of God, let us hold fast our profession. For we have not an high priest which cannot be touched with the feeling of our infirmities; but was in all points tempted like as we are, yet without sin. Let us therefore come boldly unto the throne of grace, that we may obtain mercy, and find grace to help in time of need.

Hebrews 4:14–16

We have known and believed the love that God hath to us. God is love; and he that dwelleth in love dwelleth in God, and God in him. Herein is our love made perfect, that we may have boldness in the day of judgment: because as he is, so are we in this world.

1 John 4:16–17

The LORD is my light and my salvation; whom shall I fear? the LORD is the strength of my life; of whom shall I be afraid?

Psalm 27:1

I know that this shall turn to my salvation through your prayer, and the supply of the Spirit of Jesus Christ. According to my earnest expectation and my hope, that in nothing I shall be ashamed, but that with all boldness, as always, so now also Christ shall be magnified in my body, whether it be by life, or by death. For to me to live is Christ, and to die is gain.

Philippians 1:19–21

The wicked flee when no man pursueth: but the righteous are bold as a lion.

Proverbs 28:1

Who is as the wise man? and who knoweth the interpretation of a thing? a man's wisdom maketh his face to shine, and the boldness of his face shall be changed.

Ecclesiastes 8:1

CELEBRATION

Behold, God is my salvation; I will trust, and
not be afraid: for the LORD JEHOVAH is my
strength and my song; he also is become my
salvation. Therefore with joy shall ye draw
water out of the wells of salvation. And in
that day shall ye say, Praise the LORD, call
upon his name, declare his doings among the
people, make mention that his name is
exalted. Sing unto the LORD; for he hath
done excellent things: this is known in all the
earth. Cry out and shout, thou inhabitant of
Zion: for great is the Holy One of Israel in
the midst of thee.

Isaiah 12:2–6

I will sing unto the LORD, for he hath
triumphed gloriously. ... The LORD is my
strength and song, and he is become my
salvation: he is my God, and I will prepare
him an habitation; my father's God, and I
will exalt him.

Exodus 15:1–2

Let them praise his name in the dance: let
them sing praises unto him with the timbrel
and harp. For the LORD taketh pleasure in
his people: he will beautify the meek
with salvation.

Psalm 149:3–4

"Behold, I create new heavens and a new
earth: and the former shall not be
remembered, nor come into mind. Be ye glad
and rejoice for ever in that which I create:
for, behold, I create Jerusalem a rejoicing,
and her people a joy. And I will rejoice in
Jerusalem, and joy in my people: and the
voice of weeping shall be no more heard in
her, nor the voice of crying," saith the Lord.

Isaiah 65:17–19

I have set the LORD always before me:
because he is at my right hand, I shall not
be moved. Therefore my heart is glad, and
my glory rejoiceth: my flesh also shall rest
in hope.

Psalm 16:8–9

CHALLENGE

Being justified by faith, we have peace with God through our Lord Jesus Christ: By whom also we have access by faith into this grace wherein we stand, and rejoice in hope of the glory of God. And not only so, but we glory in tribulations also: knowing that tribulation worketh patience; And patience, experience; and experience, hope: and hope maketh not ashamed; because the love of God is shed abroad in our hearts by the Holy Ghost which is given unto us.

Romans 5:1–5

When thou passest through the waters, I will be with thee; and through the rivers, they shall not overflow thee: when thou walkest through the fire, thou shalt not be burned; neither shall the flame kindle upon thee. For I am the LORD thy God, the Holy One of Israel, thy Saviour.

Isaiah 43:2–3

Wherefore seeing we also are compassed
about with so great a cloud of witnesses, let
us lay aside every weight, and the sin which
doth so easily beset us, and let us run with
patience the race that is set before us,
Looking unto Jesus the author and finisher of
our faith; who for the joy that was set before
him endured the cross, despising the shame,
and is set down at the right hand of the
throne of God.

Hebrews 12:1–2

The LORD GOD will help me; therefore shall
I not be confounded: therefore have I
set my face like a flint, and I know that I
shall not be ashamed.

Isaiah 50:7

CHILDREN

Jesus called a little child unto him, and set him in the midst of them, ... [and] Jesus said, "Whosoever therefore shall humble himself as this little child, the same is greatest in the kingdom of heaven."

Matthew 18:2, 4

Children are an heritage of the LORD and the fruit of the womb is his reward. As arrows are in the hand of a mighty man; so are children of the youth. Happy is the man that hath his quiver full of them.

Psalm 127: 3–5

God will love thee, and bless thee, and multiply thee: he will also bless the fruit of thy womb, and the fruit of thy land.

Deuteronomy 7:13

The children of God's servants shall continue, and their seed shall be established before thee.

Psalm 102:28

Children's children are the crown of old men;
and the glory of children are their fathers.

Proverbs 17:6

Children, obey your parents in the Lord: for
this is right. Honour thy father and mother;
which is the first commandment with
promise; That it may be well with thee, and
thou mayest live long on the earth.

Ephesians 6:1–3

Blessed is every one that feareth the LORD;
that walketh in his ways. For thou shalt eat
the labour of thine hands: happy shalt thou
be, and it shall be well with thee. ... Thy
children [shall be] like olive plants round
about thy table. Behold, that thus shall the
man be blessed that feareth the LORD.

Psalm 128:1–4

All thy children shall be taught of the LORD;
and great shall be the peace of thy children.

Isaiah 54:13

COMFORT

Blessed be God, even the Father of our Lord Jesus Christ, the Father of mercies, and the God of all comfort; Who comforteth us in all our tribulation, that we may be able to comfort them which are in any trouble, by the comfort wherewith we ourselves are comforted of God. As the sufferings of Christ abound in us, so our consolation also aboundeth by Christ.

2 Corinthians 1:3–5

Though I walk in the midst of trouble, thou wilt revive me, O Lord: thou shalt stretch forth thine hand against the wrath of mine enemies, and thy right hand shall save me.

Psalm 138:7

Yea, though I walk through the valley of the shadow of death, I will fear no evil: for thou art with me, O LORD; thy rod and thy staff they comfort me.

Psalm 23:4

The beloved of the LORD shall dwell in
safety by him; and the LORD shall cover him
all the day long, and he shall dwell between
his shoulders.

Deuteronomy 33:12

The LORD is nigh unto them that are of a
broken heart; and saveth such as be of a
contrite spirit.

Psalm 34:18

The LORD also will be a refuge for the
oppressed, a refuge in times of trouble.

Psalm 9:9

Jesus said, "I will not leave you comfortless: I
will come to you. Yet a little while, and the
world seeth me no more; but ye see me:
because I live, ye shall live also."

John 14:18–19

We know that all things work together for
good to them that love God, to them who are
the called according to his purpose.

Romans 8:28

Jesus said, "The Comforter, which is the
Holy Ghost, whom the Father will send in
my name, he shall teach you all things, and
bring all things to your remembrance,
whatsoever I have said unto you."

John 14:26

"As one whom his mother comforteth, so will
I comfort you," saith the Lord.

Isaiah 66:13

I had fainted, unless I had believed to see the
goodness of the LORD in the land of the
living. Wait on the LORD: be of good courage,
and he shall strengthen thine heart: wait, I
say, on the LORD.

Psalm 27:13–14

Behold, the Lord God will come with strong
hand, and his arm shall rule for him: behold,
his reward is with him, and his work before
him. He shall feed his flock like a shepherd:
he shall gather the lambs with his arm, and
carry them in his bosom, and shall gently
lead those that are with young.

Isaiah 40:10–11

Jesus said, "If ye love me, keep my
commandments. And I will pray the Father,
and he shall give you another Comforter, that
he may abide with you for ever."

John 14:15–16

COMMITMENT

Look to yourselves, that we lose not those
things which we have wrought, but that we
receive a full reward. ... He that abideth in
the doctrine of Christ, he hath both the
Father and the Son.

2 John 8–9

Be strong ... and let not your hands be weak:
for your work shall be rewarded.

2 Chronicles 15:7

Let us not be weary in well doing: for in due
season we shall reap, if we faint not.

Galatians 6:9

Be obedient to them that are your masters ...
Not with eyeservice, as menpleasers; but as
the servants of Christ, doing the will of God
from the heart; with good will doing service,
as to the Lord, and not to men: knowing that
whatsoever good thing any man doeth, the
same shall he receive of the Lord.

Ephesians 6:5–8

Delight thyself also in the LORD; and he shall give thee the desires of thine heart. Commit thy way unto the LORD; trust also in him; and he shall bring it to pass.

Psalm 37:4–5

Prove all things; hold fast that which is good. ... And the very God of peace sanctify you wholly; and I pray God your whole spirit and soul and body be preserved blameless unto the coming of our Lord Jesus Christ. Faithful is he that calleth you, who also will do it.

1 Thessalonians 5:21, 23–24

Jesus said, "Behold, I come quickly: hold that fast which thou hast, that no man take thy crown. Him that overcometh will I make a pillar in the temple of my God, and he shall go no more out: and I will write upon him the name of my God, and the name of the city of my God, which is new Jerusalem, which cometh down out of heaven from my God: and I will write upon him my new name."

Revelation 3:11–12

COMMUNICATION

He that keepeth his mouth keepeth his life.

Proverbs 13:3

Confess your faults one to another, and pray one for another, that ye may be healed. The effectual fervent prayer of a righteous man availeth much.

James 5:16

The mouth of the righteous speaketh wisdom, and his tongue talketh of judgment. The law of his God is in his heart; none of his steps shall slide.

Psalm 37:30–31

Be no more children, tossed to and fro, and carried about with every wind of doctrine, by the sleight of men, and cunning craftiness, whereby they lie in wait to deceive; But speaking the truth in love, may grow up into him in all things, which is the head, even Christ.

Ephesians 4:14–15

A wholesome tongue is a tree of life.

Proverbs 15:4

He that refraineth his lips is wise. The
tongue of the just is as choice silver.

Proverbs 10:19—20

A soft answer turneth away wrath: but
grievous words stir up anger. The tongue of
the wise useth knowledge aright.

Proverbs 15:1—2

The Lord GOD hath given me the tongue of
the learned, that I should know how to speak
a word in season to him that is weary.

Isaiah 50:4

The heart of the wise teacheth his mouth,
and addeth learning to his lips. Pleasant
words are as an honeycomb, sweet to the
soul, and health to the bones.

Proverbs 16:23—24

COMPASSION

God will turn again, he will have compassion upon us; he will subdue our iniquities; and thou wilt cast all their sins into the depths of the sea.

Micah 7:19

The LORD hath made his wonderful works to be remembered: the LORD is gracious and full of compassion.

Psalm 111:4

We count them happy which endure. Ye have heard of the patience of Job, and have seen the end of the Lord; that the Lord is very pitiful, and of tender mercy.

James 5:11

The LORD is good to all: and his tender mercies are over all his works.

Psalm 145:9

Thou art a God ready to pardon, gracious and merciful, slow to anger, and of great kindness.

Nehemiah 9:17

Unto the upright there ariseth light in the darkness: God is gracious, and full of compassion, and righteous.

Psalm 112:4

Like as a father pitieth his children, so the LORD pitieth them that fear him.

Psalm 103:13

The mountains shall depart, and the hills be removed; but my kindness shall not depart from thee, neither shall the covenant of my peace be removed, saith the LORD that hath mercy on thee.

Isaiah 54:10

"Can a woman forget her sucking child, that she should not have compassion on the son of her womb? yea, they may forget, yet will I not forget thee. Behold, I have graven thee upon the palms of my hands; thy walls are continually before me," saith the Lord.

Isaiah 49:15—16

Great are thy tender mercies, O LORD:
quicken me according to thy judgments.

Psalm 119:156

Thou, O Lord, art a God full of compassion,
and gracious, longsuffering, and plenteous in
mercy and truth.

Psalm 86:15

He that hath pity upon the poor lendeth
unto the LORD; and that which he hath given
will he pay him again.

Proverbs 19:17

God is not unrighteous to forget your work
and labour of love, which ye have showed
toward his name, in that ye have ministered
to the saints, and do minister.

Hebrews 6:10

If ye turn again unto the LORD, your
brethren and your children shall find
compassion before them that lead them
captive, so that they shall come again into
this land: for the LORD your God is gracious
and merciful, and will not turn away his face
from you, if ye return unto him.

2 Chronicles 30:9

CONFIDENCE

Cast not away ... your confidence, which
hath great recompence of reward. For ye have
need of patience, that, after ye have done the
will of God, ye might receive the promise.

Hebrews 10:35

The work of righteousness shall be peace;
and the effect of righteousness quietness and
assurance for ever.

Isaiah 32:17

We may boldly say, The Lord is my helper,
and I will not fear what man shall do
unto me.

Hebrews 13:6

The LORD is my light and my salvation;
whom shall I fear? the LORD is the strength
of my life; of whom shall I be afraid? ...
Though an host should encamp against me,
my heart shall not fear: though war should
rise against me, in this will I be confident.

Psalm 27:1, 3

The name of the LORD is a strong tower: the righteous runneth into it, and is safe.

Proverbs 18:10

Truly my soul waiteth upon God: from him cometh my salvation. He only is my rock and my salvation; he is my defence; I shall not be greatly moved.

Psalm 62:1–2

The LORD shall be thy confidence, and shall keep thy foot from being taken.

Proverbs 3:26

Blessed is the man that trusteth in the LORD, and whose hope the LORD is. For he shall be as a tree planted by the waters, and that spreadeth out her roots by the river, and shall not see when heat cometh, but her leaf shall be green; and shall not be careful in the year of drought, neither shall cease from yielding fruit.

Jeremiah 17:7–8

In the fear of the LORD is strong confidence:
and his children shall have a place of refuge.

Proverbs 14:26

Jesus said, "My grace is sufficient for thee: for
my strength is made perfect in weakness."

2 Corinthians 12:9

Beloved, if our heart condemn us not, then
have we confidence toward God. And
whatsoever we ask, we receive of him,
because we keep his commandments, and do
those things that are pleasing in his sight.

1 John 3:21—22

The LORD is my rock, and my fortress, and
my deliverer; my God, my strength, in whom
I will trust; my buckler, and the horn of my
salvation, and my high tower. I will call upon
the LORD, who is worthy to be praised: so
shall I be saved from mine enemies.

Psalm 18:2—3

Shall every one that is godly pray unto thee
in a time when thou mayest be found: surely
in the floods of great waters they shall not
come nigh unto him. Thou are my hiding
place; thou shalt preserve me from trouble;
thou shalt compass me about with songs of
deliverance.

Psalm 32:6–7

This is the confidence that we have in Christ,
that, if we ask any thing according to his will,
he heareth us: and if we know that he hear
us, whatsoever we ask, we know that we have
the petitions that we desired of him.

1 John 5:14

CONFUSION

"I will instruct thee and teach thee in the way
which thou shalt go: I will guide thee with
mine eye," saith the Lord.

Psalm 32:8

Then spake Jesus, saying, "I am the light of
the world: he that followeth me shall not
walk in darkness, but shall have the light
of life."

John 8:12

"I will bring the blind by a way that they
knew not; I will lead them in paths that they
have not known: I will make darkness light
before them, and crooked things straight.
These things will I do unto them, and not
forsake them," saith the Lord.

Isaiah 42:16

God is not the author of confusion, but of
peace, as in all churches of the saints.

1 Corinthians 14:33

Jesus said, "Peace I leave with you, my peace
I give unto you: not as the world giveth, give
I unto you. Let not your heart be troubled,
neither let it be afraid."

John 14:27

If any of you lack wisdom, let him ask of
God, that giveth to all men liberally and
upbraideth not; and it shall be given him.

James 1:5

In thee, O LORD, do I put my trust: let me
never be put to confusion.

Psalm 71:1

CONTENTMENT

Let your conversation be without covetousness; and be content with such things as ye have: for Jesus hath said, I will never leave thee, nor forsake thee.

Hebrews 13:5

I have learned, in whatsoever state I am, therewith to be content. I know both how to be abased, and I know how to abound: every where and in all things I am instructed both to be full and to be hungry, both to abound and to suffer need. I can do all things through Christ which strengtheneth me.

Philippians 4:11–13

Better is little with the fear of the LORD than great treasure and trouble therewith.

Proverbs 15:16

Better is an handful with quietness, than both the hands full with travail and vexation of spirit.

Ecclesiastes 4:6

Let not thine heart envy sinners: but be thou in the fear of the LORD all the day long. For surely there is an end; and thine expectation shall not be cut off.

Proverbs 23:17–18

The little that a righteous man hath is better than the riches of many wicked. For the arms of the wicked shall be broken: but the LORD upholdeth the righteous.

Psalm 37:16–17

The fear of the LORD tendeth to life: and he that hath it shall abide satisfied; he shall not be visited with evil.

Proverbs 19:23

Better is a little with righteousness than great revenues without right.

Proverbs 16:8

COURAGE

O love the LORD, all ye his saints: for the
LORD preserveth the faithful, and plentifully
rewardeth the proud doer. Be of good
courage, and he shall strengthen your heart,
all ye that hope in the LORD.

Psalm 31:23–24

The LORD is my light and my salvation;
whom shall I fear? The LORD is the strength
of my life; of whom shall I be afraid? When
the wicked, even mine enemies and my foes,
came upon me to eat up my flesh, they
stumbled and fell. Though an host should
encamp against me, my heart shall not fear:
though war should rise against me, in this
will I be confident.

Psalm 27:1–3

Be strong and of a good courage, fear not,
nor be afraid: ... for the LORD, thy God, he it
is that doth go with thee; he will not fail thee,
nor forsake thee.

Deuteronomy 31:6

The LORD is my strength and my shield; my
heart trusted in him, and I am helped:
therefore my heart greatly rejoiceth; and with
my song will I praise him.

Psalm 28:7

It is God that girdeth me with strength, and
maketh my way perfect. He maketh my feet
like hinds' feet, and setteth me upon my
high places.

Psalm 18:32–33

God wilt light my candle: the LORD my God
will enlighten my darkness. By thee I have
run through a troop; and by my God have I
leaped over a wall.

Psalm 18:28–29

The Lord GOD will help me; therefore shall I
not be confounded: therefore have I set my
face like a flint, and I know that I shall not
be ashamed.

Isaiah 50:7

Fear thou not; for I am with thee: be not dismayed; for I am thy God: I will strengthen thee; yea, I will help thee; yea, I will uphold thee with the right hand of my righteousness.

Isaiah 41:10

What time I am afraid, I will trust in thee. In God I will praise his word, in God I have put my trust; I will not fear what flesh can do unto me.

Psalm 56:3–4

In the time of trouble God shall hide me in his pavilion: in the secret of his tabernacle shall he hide me; he shall set me up upon a rock.

Psalm 27:5

Be not afraid of sudden fear, neither of the desolation of the wicked, when it cometh. For the LORD shall be thy confidence, and shall keep thy foot from being taken.

Proverbs 3:25–26

DESPAIR

The LORD is nigh unto them that are of a
broken heart; and saveth such as be of a
contrite spirit.

Psalm 34:18

Hope maketh not ashamed; because the love
of God is shed abroad in our hearts by the
Holy Ghost which is given unto us.

Romans 5:5

The LORD, he it is that doth go before thee;
he will be with thee, he will not fail thee,
neither forsake thee: fear not, neither
be dismayed.

Deuteronomy 31:8

Thus saith the high and lofty One that
inhabiteth eternity, whose name is Holy; I
dwell in the high and holy place, with him
also that is of a contrite and humble spirit, to
revive the spirit of the humble, and to revive
the heart of the contrite ones.

Isaiah 57:15

This I recall to my mind, therefore have I hope. It is of the LORD's mercies that we are not consumed, because his compassions fail not. They are new every morning: great is thy faithfulness. The Lord is my portion, saith my soul; therefore will I hope in him.

Lamentations 3:21—24

A bruised reed shall God not break, and the smoking flax shall he not quench.

Isaiah 42:3

We are troubled on every side, yet not distressed; we are perplexed, but not in despair; Persecuted, but not forsaken; cast down, but not destroyed; Always bearing about in the body the dying of the Lord Jesus, that the life also of Jesus might be made manifest in our body. For we which live are always delivered unto death for Jesus' sake, that the life also of Jesus might be made manifest in our mortal flesh.

2 Corinthians 4:8—11

DISAPPOINTMENT

Why art thou cast down, O my soul? and
why art thou disquieted within me? hope in
God: for I shall yet praise him, who is the
health of my countenance, and my God.

Psalm 43:5

Be ye strong,… and let not your hands be
weak: for your work shall be rewarded.

2 Chronicles 15:7

Then I said, I have laboured in vain, I have
spent my strength for nought, and in vain:
yet surely my judgment is with the LORD,
and my work with my God.

Isaiah 49:4

Jesus said, "Blessed are you who hunger now,
for you will be satisfied. Blessed are ye who
weep now, for ye shall laugh."

Luke 6:21

God healeth the broken in heart, and
bindeth up their wounds.

Psalm 147:3

[God's people] shall not labour in vain, nor
bring forth for trouble; for they *are* the seed
of the blessed of the LORD, and their
offspring with them.

Isaiah 65:23

The Lord will not cast off his people, neither
will he forsake his inheritance. But judgment
shall return unto righteousness: and all the
upright in heart shall follow it.

Psalm 94:14–15

DISCERNMENT

Whoso keepeth the commandment shall feel no evil thing: and a wise man's heart discerneth both time and judgment.

Ecclesiastes 8:5

The natural man receiveth not the things of the Spirit of God: for they are foolishness unto him: neither can he know them, because they are spiritually discerned. But he that is spiritual judgeth all things, yet he himself is judged of no man. For who hath known the mind of the Lord, that he may instruct him? But we have the mind of Christ.

1 Corinthians 2:14–16

We are of God: he that knoweth God heareth us; he that is not of God heareth not us. Hereby know we the spirit of truth, and the spirit of error.

1 John 4:6

Thine ears shall hear a word behind thee, saying, This is the way, walk ye in it, when ye turn to the right hand, and when ye turn to the left.

Isaiah 30:21

The wisdom that is from above is first pure, then peaceable, gentle, and easy to be entreated, full of mercy and good fruits, without partiality, and without hypocrisy. And the fruit of righteousness is sown in peace of them that make peace.

James 3:17—18

Hear ... and receive my sayings; and the years of thy life shall be many. I have taught thee in the way of wisdom; I have led thee in right paths. When thou goest, thy steps shall not be straitened; and when thou runnest, thou shalt not stumble. Take fast hold of instruction; let her not go: keep her; for she is thy life.

Proverbs 4:10—13

Be strong in the grace that is in Christ Jesus. And the things that thou hast heard of me among many witnesses, the same commit thou to faithful men, who shall be able to teach others also. ... Consider what I say; and the Lord give thee understanding in all things.

2 Timothy 2:1—2, 7

DISCIPLESHIP

Then said Jesus to those Jews which believed on him, If ye continue in my word, then are ye my disciples indeed; and ye shall know the truth, and the truth shall make you free.

John 8:31–32

Jesus said, "I am the vine, ye are the branches: He that abideth in me, and I in him, the same bringeth forth much fruit: for without me ye can do nothing."

John 15:5

He that soweth to his flesh shall of the flesh reap corruption; but he that soweth to the spirit shall of the Spirit reap life everlasting.

Galatians 6:8

Jesus said, "By this shall all men know that ye are my disciples, if ye have love one to another."

John 13:35

Jesus said, "He that hath my commandments, and keepeth them, he it is that loveth me: and he that loveth me shall be loved of my Father, and I will love him, and will manifest myself to him."

John 14:21

Jesus said, "If any man serve me, let him follow me; and where I am, there shall also my servant be: if any man serve me, him will my Father honour."

John 12:26

Then spake Jesus, saying, "I am the light of the world: he that followeth me shall not walk in darkness, but shall have the light of life."

John 8:12

Jesus said, "He that findeth his life shall lose it: and he that loseth his life for my sake shall find it."

Matthew 10:39

DISCIPLINE

Blessed is the man whom thou chastenest, O LORD, and teachest him out of thy law.

Psalm 94:12

Despise not thou the chastening of the Lord, nor faint when thou art rebuked of him: For whom the Lord loveth he chasteneth, and scourgeth every son whom he receiveth. If ye endure chastening, God dealeth with you as with sons.

Hebrews 12:5—7

Correct thy son, and he shall give thee rest; yea, he shall give delight unto thy soul.

Proverbs 29:17

The ear that heareth the reproof of life abideth among the wise. He that refuseth instruction despiseth his own soul: but he that heareth reproof getteth understanding.

Proverbs 15:31—32

No chastening for the present seemeth to be joyous, but grievous: nevertheless afterward it yieldeth the peaceable fruit of righteousness unto them which are exercised thereby.

Hebrews 12:11

Train up a child in the way he should go: and when he is old, he will not depart from it.

Proverbs 22:6

Hear counsel, and receive instruction, that thou mayest be wise in thy latter end. There are many devices in a man's heart; nevertheless the counsel of the LORD, that shall stand.

Proverbs 19:20—21

Despise not the chastening of the LORD; neither be weary of his correction: For whom the LORD loveth he correcteth; even as a father the son in whom he delighteth.

Proverbs 3:11—12

ENCOURAGEMENT

The liberal soul shall be made fat: and he that watereth shall be watered also himself.

Proverbs 11:25

Our Lord Jesus Christ himself, and God, even our Father, which hath loved us, and hath given us everlasting consolation and good hope through grace, Comfort your hearts, and stablish you in every good word and work.

2 Thessalonians 2:16–17

Though our outward man perish, yet the inward man is renewed day by day. For our light affliction, which is but for a moment, worketh for us a far more exceeding and eternal weight of glory.

2 Corinthians 4:16–17

Unto thee, O LORD, do I lift up my soul. O my God, I trust in thee: let me not be ashamed.

Psalm 25:1–2

This I recall to my mind, therefore have I
hope. It is of the LORD's mercies that we are
not consumed, because his compassions fail
not. They are new every morning: great is
thy faithfulness.

Lamentations 3:21—23

Blessed be the LORD, who daily loadeth us
with benefits, even the God of our salvation.

Psalm 68:19

Jesus said, "These things I have spoken unto
you, that in me ye might have peace. In the
world ye shall have tribulation: but be of
good cheer; I have overcome the world."

John 16:33

EVANGELISM

I am not ashamed of the gospel of Christ: for
it is the power of God unto salvation to every
one that believeth.

Romans 1:16

Jesus said, "The gospel must ... be published
among all nations. But when they shall lead
· you, and deliver you up, take no thought
beforehand what ye shall speak, neither do ye
premeditate: but whatsoever shall be given
you in that hour, that speak ye: for it is not ye
that speak, but the Holy Ghost."

Mark 13:10—11

Jesus said, "All power is given unto me in
heaven and in earth. Go ye therefore, and
teach all nations, baptizing them in the name
of the Father, and of the Son, and of the
Holy Ghost: Teaching them to observe all
things whatsoever I have commanded you:
and, lo, I am with you always, even unto the
end of the world."

Matthew 28:18—20

Let your light so shine before men, that they may see your good works, and glorify your Father which is in heaven.

Matthew 5:16

He that shall endure unto the end, the same shall be saved. This gospel of the kingdom shall be preached in all the world for a witness unto all nations; and then shall the end come.

Matthew 24:13–14

God so loved the world, that he gave his only begotten Son, that whosoever believeth in him should not perish, but have everlasting life. For God sent not his Son into the world to condemn the world; but that the world through him might be saved.

John 3:16–17

EVERLASTING LIFE

Jesus said, "This is the will of him that sent me, that every one which seeth the Son, and believeth on him, may have everlasting life: and I will raise him up at the last day."

John 6:40

The Father loveth the son, and hath given all things into his hand. He that believeth on the Son hath everlasting life.

John 3:35–36

Jesus said, "Verily, verily, I say unto you, He that heareth my word, and believeth on him that sent me, hath everlasting life, and shall not come into condemnation; but is passed from death unto life."

John 5:24

The world passeth away, and the lust thereof: but he that doeth the will of God abideth for ever.

1 John 2:17

Being made free from sin, and become servants to God, ye have your fruit unto holiness, and the end everlasting life. For the wages of sin is death; but the gift of God is eternal life through Jesus Christ our Lord.

Romans 6:22–23

These words spake Jesus, and lifted up his eyes to heaven, and said, "Father, the hour is come; glorify thy Son, that thy Son also may glorify thee: As thou hast given him power over all flesh, that he should give eternal life to as many as thou hast given him. And this is life eternal, that they might know thee the only true God, and Jesus Christ, whom thou hast sent."

John 17:1–3

Jesus said, "My sheep hear my voice, and I know them, and they follow me: and I give unto them eternal life; and they shall never perish, neither shall any man pluck them out of my hand. My Father, which gave them me, is greater than all; and no man is able to pluck them out of my Father's hand. I and my Father are one."

John 10:27–30

FAITH

Jesus said, "If ye have faith as a grain of mustard seed, ye shall say unto this mountain, Remove hence to yonder place; and it shall remove; and nothing shall be impossible unto you."

Matthew 17:20

Whatsoever is born of God overcometh the world: and this is the victory that overcometh the world, *even* our faith. Who is he that overcometh the world, but he that believeth that Jesus is the Son of God?

1 John 5:4–5

Ye are all the children of God by faith in Christ Jesus.

Galatians 3:26

Without faith it is impossible to please God: for he that cometh to God must believe that he is, and that he is a rewarder of them that diligently seek him.

Hebrews 11:6

Jesus said, "If thou canst believe, all things are possible to him that believeth."

Mark 9:23

Being justified by faith, we have peace with God through our Lord Jesus Christ: By whom also we have access by faith into this grace wherein we stand, and rejoice in hope of the glory of God.

Romans 5:1–2

Jesus said, "Verily, verily, I say unto you, He that believeth on me, the works that I do shall he do also; and greater works than these shall he do; because I go unto my Father."

John 14:12

By grace are ye saved through faith; and that not of yourselves: it is the gift of God: Not of works, lest any man should boast.

Ephesians 2:8–9

The righteousness of God revealed from faith to faith: as it is written, The just shall live by faith.

Romans 1:17

FAITHFULNESS

Know therefore that the LORD thy God, he is
God, the faithful God, which keepeth
covenant and mercy with them that love him
and keep his commandments to a thousand
generations.

Deuteronomy 7:9

"My lovingkindness will I not utterly take
from him, nor suffer my faithfulness to fail.
My covenant will I not break, nor alter the
thing that is gone out of my lips," saith
the Lord.

Psalm 89:33–34

O love the LORD, all ye his saints: for the
LORD preserveth the faithful, and plentifully
rewardeth the proud doer.

Psalm 31:23

The LORD loveth judgment, and forsaketh
not his saints; they are preserved for ever.

Psalm 37:28

God layeth up sound wisdom for the
righteous: he is a buckler to them that walk
uprightly. He keepeth the paths of judgment,
and preserveth the way of his saints.

Proverbs 2:7–8

God is faithful, by whom ye were called
unto the fellowship of his Son Jesus Christ
our Lord.

1 Corinthians 1:9

He that is faithful in that which is least is
faithful also in much.

Luke 16:10

FAMILY

Jesus took not on him the nature of angels;
but he took on him the seed of Abraham.
Wherefore in all things it behooved him to
be made like unto his brethren, that he might
be a merciful and faithful high priest in
things pertaining to God, to make
reconciliation for the sins of the people. For
in that he himself hath suffered being
tempted, he is able to succour them that
are tempted.

Hebrews 2:16—18

Behold, how good and how pleasant it is for
brethren to dwell together in unity!

Psalm 133:1

Behold, what manner of love the Father hath
bestowed upon us, that we should be called
the sons of God: therefore the world
knoweth us not, because it knew him not.
Beloved, now are we the sons of God, and it
doth not yet appear what we shall be: but we
know that, when he shall appear, we shall be
like him; for we shall see him as he is.

1 John 3:1—2

I will receive you, and will be a Father unto
you, and ye shall be my sons and daughters,
saith the Lord Almighty.

2 Corinthians 6:17–18

I bow my knees unto the Father of our Lord
Jesus Christ, of whom the whole family in
heaven and earth is named, That he would
grant you, according to the riches of his glory,
to be strengthened with might by his Spirit
in the inner man.

Ephesians 3:14–16

God setteth the poor on high from affliction,
and maketh him families like a flock. The
righteous shall see it, and rejoice: and all
iniquity shall stop her mouth. Whoso is wise,
and will observe these things, even they shall
understand the lovingkindness of the LORD.

Psalm 107:41–43

FELLOWSHIP

If we walk in the light, as God is in the light,
we have fellowship one with another, and the
blood of Jesus Christ his Son cleanseth us
from all sin.

1 John 1:7

God is faithful, by whom ye were called
unto the fellowship of his Son Jesus Christ
our Lord.

1 Corinthians 1:9

If two lie together, then they have heat: but
how can one be warm alone? And if one
prevail against him, two shall withstand him;
and a threefold cord is not quickly broken.

Ecclesiastes 4:11

If we love one another, God dwelleth in us,
and his love is perfected in us. Hereby know
we that we dwell in him, and he in us,
because he hath given us of his Spirit.

1 John 4:12–13

Jesus said, "Where two or three are gathered together in my name, there am I in the midst of them."

Matthew 18:20

That which we have seen and heard declare we unto you, that ye also may have fellowship with us: and truly our fellowship is with the Father, and with his Son Jesus Christ. And these things write we unto you, that your joy may be full.

1 John 1:3—4

Let us consider one another to provoke unto love and to good works: Not forsaking the assembling of ourselves together, as the manner of some is; but exhorting one another: and so much the more, as ye see the day approaching.

Hebrews 10:24—25

FINANCES

Wealth gotten by vanity shall be
diminished: but he that gathereth by
labour shall increase.

Proverbs 13:11

My God shall supply all your need according
to his riches in glory by Christ Jesus.

Philippians 4:19

Jesus said, "Take no thought, saying, What
shall we eat? or, What shall we drink? or,
Wherewithal shall we be clothed? ... for your
heavenly Father knoweth that ye have need
of all these things. But seek ye first the
kingdom of God, and his righteousness; and
all these things shall be added unto you."

Matthew 6:31–33

Praise ye the LORD. Blessed is the man that feareth the LORD, that delighteth greatly in his commandments.... Wealth and riches shall be in his house: and his righteousness endureth for ever.

Psalm 112:1, 3

The substance of a diligent man is precious.

Proverbs 12:27

A good man leaveth an inheritance to his children's children: and the wealth of the sinner is laid up for the just.

Proverbs 13:22

FORGIVENESS

If we confess our sins, God is faithful and just to forgive us our sins, and to cleanse us from all unrighteousness.

1 John 1:9

As far as the east is from the west, so far hath God removed our transgressions from us.

Psalm 103:12

Who is a God like unto thee, that pardoneth iniquity, and passeth by the transgression of the remnant of his heritage? he retaineth not his anger for ever, because he delighteth in mercy.

Micah 7:18

Jesus said, "If ye forgive men their trespasses, your heavenly Father will also forgive you."

Matthew 6:14

Come now, and let us reason together, saith the LORD: though your sins be as scarlet, they shall be as white as snow; though they be red like crimson, they shall be as wool.

Isaiah 1:18

"I, even I, am he that blotteth out thy transgressions for mine own sake, and will not remember thy sins," saith the Lord.

Isaiah 43:25

You, being dead in your sins and the uncircumcision of your flesh, hath God quickened together with Christ, having forgiven you all trespasses; blotting out the handwriting of ordinances that was against us, which was contrary to us, and took it out of the way, nailing it to his cross.

Colossians 2:13—14

Blessed is he whose transgression is forgiven, whose sin is covered.

Psalm 32:1

Thou, Lord, art good, and ready to forgive;
and plenteous in mercy unto all them that
call upon thee.

Psalm 86:5

He that covereth a transgression
seeketh love.

Proverbs 17:9

"I will cleanse them from all their iniquity,
whereby they have sinned against me; and I
will pardon all their iniquities, whereby they
have sinned, and whereby they have
transgressed against me," saith the Lord.

Jeremiah 33:8

Thou art a God ready to pardon,
gracious and merciful, slow to anger, and
of great kindness.

Nehemiah 9:17

FREEDOM

The Lord himself shall descend from heaven
with a shout, with the voice of the archangel,
and with the trump of God: and the dead in
Christ shall rise first: Then we which are
alive and remain shall be caught up together
with them in the clouds, to meet the Lord in
the air: and so shall we ever be with the Lord.

1 Thessalonians 4:16—17

Knowing this, that our old man is crucified
with Christ, that the body of sin might be
destroyed, that henceforth we should not
serve sin. For he that is dead is freed
from sin.

Romans 6:6—7

Jesus said, "Verily, verily, I say unto you,
Whosoever committeth sin is the servant of
sin. And the servant abideth not in the house
for ever: but the Son abideth ever. If the Son
therefore shall make you free, ye shall be
free indeed."

John 8:34—36

Being made free from sin, and become
servants to God, ye have your fruit unto
holiness, and the end everlasting life.

Romans 6:22

The law of the Spirit of life in Christ Jesus
hath made me free from the law of sin
and death.

Romans 8:2

Ye have been called unto liberty; only use not
liberty for an occasion to the flesh, but by
love serve one another.

Galatians 5:13

FRIENDSHIP

A man that hath friends must show himself
friendly: and there is a friend that sticketh
closer than a brother.

Proverbs 18:24

A friend loveth at all times, and a brother is
born for adversity.

Proverbs 17:17

Jesus saith, "Henceforth I call you not
servants; for the servant knoweth not what
his lord doeth: but I have called you friends;
for all things that I have heard of my Father I
have made known unto you."

John 15:15

Iron sharpeneth iron; so a man sharpeneth
the countenance of his friend.

Proverbs 27:17

Two are better than one; because they have a
good reward for their labour. For if they fall,
the one will lift up his fellow: but woe to him
that is alone when he falleth; for he hath not
another to help him up. Again, if two lie
together, then they have heat: but how can
one be warm alone? And if one prevail
against him, two shall withstand him; and a
threefold cord is not quickly broken.

Ecclesiastes 4:9—12

GIVING

He which soweth sparingly shall reap also sparingly; and he which soweth bountifully shall reap also bountifully. Every man according as he purposeth in his heart, so let him give; not grudgingly, or of necessity: for God loveth a cheerful giver.

2 Corinthians 9:6–7

Jesus said, "Give, and it shall be given unto you; good measure, pressed down, and shaken together, and running over, shall men give into your bosom. For with the same measure that ye mete withal it shall be measured to you again."

Luke 6:38

God spared not his own Son, but delivered him up for us all, how shall he not with him also freely give us all things?

Romans 8:32

A good man showeth favour, and lendeth: he will guide his affairs with discretion. Surely

he shall not be moved for ever: the righteous
shall be in everlasting remembrance.

Psalm 112:5–6

He that hath a bountiful eye shall be blessed;
for he giveth of his bread to the poor.

Proverbs 22:9

Charge them that are rich in this world, that
they be not highminded, nor trust in
uncertain riches, but in the living God, who
giveth us richly all things to enjoy.

1 Timothy 6:17

Bring ye all the tithes into the storehouse,
that there may be meat in mine house, and
prove me now herewith, saith the LORD of
hosts, if I will not open you the windows of
heaven, and pour you out a blessing, that
there shall not be room enough to receive it.

Malachi 3:10

It is more blessed to give than to receive.

Acts 20:35

GOD'S PRESENCE

Jesus said, "Where two or three are gathered together in my name, there am I in the midst of them."

Matthew 18:20

God said, My presence shall go with thee, and I will give thee rest.

Exodus 33:14

Jesus spake, saying, "Lo, I am with you always, even unto the end of the world."

Matthew 28:20

The LORD is nigh unto all them that call upon him, to all that call upon him in truth.

Psalm 145:18

"When thou passest through the waters, I will be with thee; and through the rivers, they shall not overflow thee: when thou walkest through the fire, thou shalt not be burned; neither shall the flame kindle upon thee," saith the Lord.

Isaiah 43:2–3

God that made the world and all things
therein, seeing that he is Lord of heaven and
earth, dwelleth not in temples made with
hands; Neither is worshipped with men's
hands, as though he needed any thing, seeing
he giveth to all life, and breath, and all things;
And hath made of one blood all nations of
men for to dwell on all the face of the earth,
and hath determined the times before
appointed, and the bounds of their
habitation; That they should seek the Lord, if
haply they might feel after him, and find him,
though he be not far from every one of us:
For in him we live, and move, and have
our being.

Acts 17:24–28

O LORD, thou hast searched me, and known
me.... If I take the wings of the morning,
and dwell in the uttermost part of the sea;
even there shall thy hand lead me, and thy
right hand shall hold me.

Psalm 139:1, 9–10

Yea, though I walk through the valley of the
shadow of death, I will fear no evil: for thou
art with me, O Lord.

Psalm 23:4

Be strong and of a good courage, fear not,
nor be afraid:... for the LORD thy God, he it
is that doth go with thee; he will not fail thee,
nor forsake thee.

Deuteronomy 31:6

GOD'S WORD

Jesus said, "It is written, Man shall not live by bread alone, but by every word that proceedeth out of the mouth of God."

Matthew 4:4

Blessed are they that hear the word of God, and keep it.

Luke 11:28

Jesus said, "Heaven and earth shall pass away: but my words shall not pass away."

Mark 13:31

Thy word is a lamp unto my feet, and a light unto my path, O Lord.

Psalm 119:105

Whatsoever things were written aforetime were written for our learning, that we through patience and comfort of the scriptures might have hope.

Romans 15:4

All scripture is given by inspiration of God,
and is profitable for doctrine, for reproof, for
correction, for instruction in righteousness:
that the man of God may be perfect,
thoroughly furnished unto all good works.

2 Timothy 3:16–17

Great peace have they which love thy law, O
Lord: and nothing shall offend them.

Psalm 119:165

In the beginning was the Word, and the
Word was with God, and the Word was God.
The same was in the beginning with God.
All things were made by him; and without
him was not any thing made that was made.
In him was life; and the life was the light
of men.

John 1:1–4

GRACE

Unto every one of us is given grace according to the measure of the gift of Christ.

Ephesians 4:7

Ye know the grace of our Lord Jesus Christ, that, though he was rich, yet for your sakes he became poor, that ye through his poverty might be rich.

2 Corinthians 8:9

Jesus said, "My grace is sufficient for thee: for my strength is made perfect in weakness."

2 Corinthians 12:9

God, who is rich in mercy, for his great love wherewith he loved us, Even when we were dead in sins, hath quickened us together with Christ, (by grace ye are saved;) and hath raised us up together, and made us sit together in heavenly places in Christ Jesus: That in the ages to come he might show the exceeding riches of his grace in his kindness toward us through Christ Jesus.

Ephesians 2:4–7

God is able to make all grace abound toward you; that ye, always having all sufficiency in all things, may abound to every good work.

2 Corinthians 9:8

By grace are ye saved through faith; and that not of yourselves: it is the gift of God: not of works, lest any man should boast.

Ephesians 2:8–9

If by one man's offence death reigned by one; much more they which receive abundance of grace and of the gift of righteousness shall reign in life by one, Jesus Christ.

Romans 5:17

Grace and peace be multiplied unto you through the knowledge of God, and of Jesus our Lord.

2 Peter 1:2

The kindness and love of God our Saviour
toward man appeared, Not by works of
righteousness which we have done, but
according to his mercy he saved us, by the
washing of regeneration, and renewing of the
Holy Ghost; Which he shed on us
abundantly through Jesus Christ our Saviour;
That being justified by his grace, we should
be made heirs according to the hope of
eternal life.

Titus 3:4–7

The God of all grace, who hath called us unto
his eternal glory by Christ Jesus, after that ye
have suffered a while, make you perfect,
stablish, strengthen, settle you.

1 Peter 5:10

I thank my God always on your behalf, for
the grace of God which is given you by Jesus
Christ; That in every thing ye are enriched by
him, in all utterance, and in all knowledge.

1 Corinthians 1:4–5

Our Lord Jesus Christ himself, and God, even our Father, which hath loved us, and hath given us everlasting consolation and good hope through grace, Comfort your hearts, and stablish you in every good word and work.

2 Thessalonians 2:16–17

Being justified by faith, we have peace with God through our Lord Jesus Christ: by whom also we have access by faith into this grace wherein we stand, and rejoice in hope of the glory of God.

Romans 5:1–2

The grace of God that bringeth salvation hath appeared to all men, Teaching us that, denying ungodliness and worldly lusts, we should live soberly, righteously, and godly, in this present world; looking for that blessed hope, and the glorious appearing of the great God and our Saviour Jesus Christ.

Titus 2:11–13

GRIEF

This is my comfort in my affliction: for thy word hath quickened me, O Lord.

Psalm 119:50

Blessed are they that mourn: for they shall be comforted.

Matthew 5:4

Jesus said, "Verily, verily, I say unto you, That ye shall weep and lament, but the world shall rejoice: and ye shall be sorrowful, but your sorrow shall be turned into joy.... Ye now therefore have sorrow: but I will see you again, and your heart shall rejoice, and your joy no man taketh from you."

John 16:20, 22

Let, I pray thee, O Lord, thy merciful kindness be for my comfort, according to thy word unto thy servant. Let thy tender mercies come unto me, that I may live: for thy law is my delight.

Psalm 119:76—77

I would not have you to be ignorant,
brethren, concerning them which are asleep,
that ye sorrow not, even as others which have
no hope. For if we believe that Jesus died and
rose again, even so them also which sleep in
Jesus will God bring with him.

1 Thessalonians 4:13—14

The LORD is nigh unto them that are of a
broken heart; and saveth such as be
of a contrite spirit.

Psalm 34:18

The ransomed of the LORD shall return, and
come to Zion with songs and everlasting joy
upon their heads: they shall obtain joy and
gladness, and sorrow and sighing shall
flee away.

Isaiah 35:10

"I have satiated the weary soul, and I have
replenished every sorrowful soul," saith
the Lord.

Jeremiah 31:25

GUIDANCE

Trust in the LORD with all thine heart; and lean not unto thine own understanding. In all thy ways acknowledge him, and he shall direct thy paths.

Proverbs 3:5–6

"I will instruct thee and teach thee in the way which thou shalt go: I will guide thee with mine eye," saith the Lord.

Psalm 32:8

This God is our God for ever and ever: he will be our guide even unto death.

Psalm 48:14

A man's heart deviseth his way: but the LORD directeth his steps.

Proverbs 16:9

The steps of a good man are ordered by the LORD: and he delighteth in his way.

Psalm 37:23

Thy word is a lamp unto my feet, and a light unto my path, O Lord.

Psalm 119:105

The LORD is my shepherd; I shall not want. He maketh me to lie down in green pastures: he leadeth me beside the still waters. He restoreth my soul: he leadeth me in the paths of righteousness for his name's sake.

Psalm 23:1–3

The LORD shall guide thee continually, and satisfy thy soul in drought, and make fat thy bones: and thou shalt be like a watered garden, and like a spring of water, whose waters fail not.

Isaiah 58:11

Thou art my rock and my fortress; therefore for thy name's sake lead me, and guide me, O Lord.

Psalm 31:3

O LORD, thou hast searched me, and known me.... If I take the wings of the morning, and dwell in the uttermost parts of the sea; Even there shall thy hand lead me, and thy right hand shall hold me.

Psalm 139:1, 9—10

Jesus said, "When he, the Spirit of truth, is come, he will guide you into all truth: for he shall not speak of himself; but whatsoever he shall hear, that shall he speak: and he will show you things to come."

John 16:13

Hear ... and receive my sayings; and the years of thy life shall be many. I have taught thee in the way of wisdom; I have led thee in right paths. When thou goest, thy steps shall not be straitened; and when thou runnest, thou shalt not stumble.

Proverbs 4:10—12

Keep thy father's commandment, and forsake
not the law of thy mother: Bind them
continually upon thine heart, and tie them
about thy neck. When thou goest, it shall
lead thee; when thou sleepest, it shall keep
thee; and when thou awakest, it shall talk
with thee.

Proverbs 6:20–22

I know the thoughts that I think toward you,
saith the LORD, thoughts of peace, and not of
evil, to give you an expected end.

Jeremiah 29:11

Thus saith the LORD, thy Redeemer, the
Holy One of Israel; I am the LORD thy God
which teacheth thee to profit, which leadeth
thee by the way that thou shouldest go.

Isaiah 48:17

GUILT

The law of the Spirit of life in Christ Jesus
hath made me free from the law of sin
and death.

Romans 8:2

Repent ye ... and be converted, that your sins
may be blotted out.

Acts 3:19

If by one man's offence death reigned by one;
much more they which receive abundance of
grace and of the gift of righteousness shall
reign in life by one, Jesus Christ.

Romans 5:17

The Lord is not slack concerning his
promise, as some men count slackness; but is
longsuffering to us-ward, not willing that any
should perish, but that all should come
to repentance.

2 Peter 3:9

Jesus said, "I say unto you, that likewise joy shall be in heaven over one sinner that repenteth, more than over ninety and nine just persons, which need no repentance."

Luke 15:7

"If the wicked will turn from all his sins that he hath committed, and keep all my statutes, and do that which is lawful and right, he shall surely live, he shall not die," saith the Lord.

Ezekiel 18:21

We know that what things soever the law saith, it saith to them who are under the law: that ... all the world may become guilty before God. ... But now the righteousness of God without the law is manifested ... even the righteousness of God which is by faith of Jesus Christ unto all and upon all them that believe.

Romans 3:19, 21–22

HAPPINESS

God giveth to a man that is good in his sight wisdom, and knowledge, and joy.

Ecclesiastes 2:26

He that despiseth his neighbour sinneth: but he that hath mercy on the poor, happy is he.

Proverbs 14:21

Thou hast turned for me my mourning into dancing, O Lord: thou hast put off my sackcloth, and girded me with gladness.

Psalm 30:11

Blessed is every one that feareth the LORD; that walketh in his ways. For thou shalt eat the labour of thine hands: happy shalt thou be, and it shall be well with thee.

Psalm 128:1–2

Thou, LORD, hast made me glad through thy work: I will triumph in the works of thy hands.

Psalm 92:4

Thou hast made known to me the ways of life; thou shalt make me full of joy with thy countenance, O God.

Acts 2:28

Happy is that people, whose God is the LORD.

Psalm 144:15

Happy is the man that finds wisdom, and the man that getteth understanding.

Proverbs 3:13

Wisdom is a tree of life to them that lay hold upon her: and happy is every one that retaineth her.

Proverbs 3:18

He that keepeth the law, happy is he.

Proverbs 29:18

If ye suffer for righteousness' sake, happy
are ye.

1 Peter 3:14

If ye be reproached for the name of Christ,
happy are ye; for the spirit of glory and of
God resteth upon you.

1 Peter 4:14

HEALTH AND HEALING

The Messiah was wounded for our
transgressions, he was bruised for our
iniquities: the chastisement of our peace was
upon him; and with his stripes we are healed.

Isaiah 53:5

"Ye shall serve the LORD your God, and he
shall bless thy bread, and thy water; and I
will take sickness away from the midst of
thee. There shall nothing cast their young,
nor be barren, in thy land: the number of thy
days I will fulfil," saith the Lord.

Exodus 23:25—26

Because Christ also suffered for us, leaving us
an example, that ye should follow his steps:
... Who his own self bare our sins in his own
body on the tree, that we, being dead to sins,
should live unto righteousness: by whose
stripes ye were healed.

1 Peter 2:21, 24

Bless the LORD, O my soul, and forget not all his benefits: Who forgiveth all thine iniquities; who healeth all thy diseases.

Psalm 103:2–3

I will restore health unto thee, and I will heal thee of thy wounds, saith the LORD.

Jeremiah 30:17

Heal me, O LORD, and I shall be healed; save me, and I shall be saved: for thou art my praise.

Jeremiah 17:14

Is any sick among you? let him call for the elders of the church; and let them pray over him, anointing him with oil in the name of the Lord: And the prayer of faith shall save the sick, and the Lord shall raise him up.

James 5:14–15

O LORD my God, I cried unto thee, and thou hast healed me.

Psalm 30:2

HEAVEN

Jesus said, "In my Father's house are many mansions: if it were not so, I would have told you. I go to prepare a place for you. And if I go and prepare a place for you, I will come again, and receive you unto myself; that where I am, there ye may be also."

John 14:2–3

Jesus said, "Verily I say unto you, Whatsoever ye shall bind on earth shall be bound in heaven: and whatsoever ye shall loose on earth shall be loosed in heaven."

Matthew 18:18

We know that if our earthly house of this tabernacle were dissolved, we have a building of God, an house not made with hands, eternal in the heavens.

2 Corinthians 5:1

Jesus said, "Behold, the kingdom of God is within you."

Luke 17:21

The kingdom of God is not meat and drink;
but righteousness, and peace, and joy in the
Holy Ghost.

Romans 14:17

Blessed be the God and Father of our Lord
Jesus Christ, which according to his
abundant mercy hath begotten us again unto
a lively hope by the resurrection of Jesus
Christ from the dead, To an inheritance
incorruptible, and undefiled, and that fadeth
not away, reserved in heaven for you, Who
are kept by the power of God through faith
unto salvation ready to be revealed in the
last time.

1 Peter 1:3–5

We have had fathers of our flesh which
corrected us, and we gave them reverence:
shall we not much rather be in subjection
unto the Father of spirits, and live? For they
verily for a few days chastened us after their
own pleasure; but he for our profit, that we
might be partakers of his holiness. Now no
chastening for the present seemeth to be
joyous, but grievous: nevertheless afterward it
yieldeth the peaceable fruit of righteousness
unto them which are exercised thereby.

Hebrews 12:9–11

Thou art holy, O thou that inhabitest the
praises of Israel.

Psalm 22:3

Give unto the LORD the glory due unto his
name; worship the LORD in the beauty
of holiness.

Psalm 29:2

The Lord make you to increase and abound
in love one toward another, and toward all
men, even as we do toward you: To the end
he may stablish your hearts unblameable in
holiness before God, even our Father, at the
coming of our Lord Jesus Christ with all
his saints.

1 Thessalonians 3:12—13

The LORD rewarded me according to my
righteousness; according to the cleanness of
my hands hath he recompensed me. For I
have kept the ways of the LORD, and have
not wickedly departed from my God.

Psalm 18:20—21

God hath chosen us in him before the
foundation of the world, that we should be
holy and without blame before him in love.

Ephesians 1:4

There is none holy as the LORD: for there is
none beside thee: neither is there any rock
like our God.

1 Samuel 2:2

Ye ... as lively stones, are built up a spiritual
house, an holy priesthood, to offer up
spiritual sacrifices, acceptable to God by
Jesus Christ.

1 Peter 2:5

You, that were sometime alienated and
enemies in your mind by wicked works, yet
now hath Christ reconciled in the body of his
flesh through death, to present you holy and
unblameable and unreproveable in his sight.

Colossians 1:21—22

The temple of God is holy, which temple
ye are.

1 Corinthians 3:17

Jesus said, "I will pray the Father, and he shall give you another Comforter, that he may abide with you for ever; Even the Spirit of truth; whom the world cannot receive, because it seeth him not, neither knoweth him: but ye know him; for he dwelleth with you, and shall be in you."

John 14:16–17

When the day of Pentecost was fully come, they were all with one accord in one place. Suddenly there came a sound from heaven as of a rushing mighty wind, and it filled all the house where they were sitting. And there appeared unto them cloven tongues like as of fire, and it sat upon each of them. And they were all filled with the Holy Ghost, and began to speak with other tongues, as the Spirit gave them utterance.

Acts 2:1–4

"It shall come to pass afterward, that I will pour out my spirit upon all flesh; and your sons and your daughters shall prophesy, your old men shall dream dreams, your young men shall see visions: and also upon the servants and upon the handmaids in those days will I pour out my spirit," declares the Lord.

Joel 2:28—29

The Spirit of the Lord GOD is upon me;... to appoint unto them that mourn in Zion, to give unto them beauty for ashes, the oil of joy for mourning, the garment of praise for the spirit of heaviness; that they might be called trees of righteousness, the planting of the LORD, that he might be glorified.

Isaiah 61:1, 3

There is therefore now no condemnation to them which are in Christ Jesus, who walk not after the flesh, but after the Spirit. For the law of the Spirit of life in Christ Jesus hath made me free from the law of sin and death.

Romans 8:1—2

The Lord is that Spirit: and where the Spirit
of the Lord is, there is liberty. But we all,
with open face beholding as in a glass the
glory of the Lord, are changed into the same
image from glory to glory, even as by the
Spirit of the Lord.

2 Corinthians 3:17—18

Jesus said, "He that believeth on me, as the
scripture hath said, out of his belly shall flow
rivers of living water." (This spake he of
the Spirit, which they that believe on him
should receive.)

John 7:38—39

Repent, and be baptized every one of you in
the name of Jesus Christ for the remission of
sins, and ye shall receive the gift of the Holy
Ghost. For the promise is unto you, and to
your children, and to all that are afar off,
even as many as the Lord our God shall call.

Acts 2:38—39

Eye hath not seen, nor ear heard, neither
have entered into the heart of man, the
things which God hath prepared for them
that love him. But God hath revealed them
unto us by his Spirit; for the Spirit searcheth
all things, yea, the deep things of God.

1 Corinthians 2:9–10

Ye are manifestly declared to be the epistle of
Christ ministered by us, written not with ink,
but with the Spirit of the living God; not in
tables of stones, but in fleshy tables of
the heart.

2 Corinthians 3:3

The fruit of the Spirit is love, joy, peace,
longsuffering, gentleness, goodness, faith,
meekness, temperance: against such there is
no law.

Galatians 5:22–23

Lying lips are abomination to the LORD: but they that deal truly are his delight.

Proverbs 12:22

Every man shall kiss his lips that giveth a right answer.

Proverbs 24:26

Brethren, whatsoever things are true, whatsoever things are honest, whatsoever things are just, whatsoever things are pure, whatsoever things are lovely, whatsoever things are of good report; if there be any virtue, and if there be any praise, think on these things. Those things, which ye have both learned, and received, and heard, and seen in me, do: and the God of peace shall be with you.

Philippians 4:8—9

He that walketh uprightly walketh surely.

Proverbs 10:9

When much people were gathered together,
and were come to Jesus out of every city, he
spake by a parable: A sower went out to sow
his seed: and as he sowed, some fell by the
way side; ... And other fell on good ground,
and sprang up, and bare fruit an hundredfold.
... Now the parable is this: The seed is the
word of God.... That on the good ground are
they, which in an honest and good heart,
having heard the word, keep it, and bring
forth fruit with patience.

Luke 8:4—5, 8, 11, 15

HOPE

The God of hope fill you with all joy and
peace in believing, that ye may abound in
hope, through the power of the Holy Ghost.

Romans 15:13

The LORD taketh pleasure in them that fear
him, in those that hope in his mercy.

Psalm 147:11

It is good that a man should both hope and
quietly wait for the salvation of the LORD.

Lamentations 3:26

Whatsoever things were written aforetime
were written for our learning, that we
through patience and comfort of the
scriptures might have hope.

Romans 15:4

Be of good courage, and God shall
strengthen your heart, all ye that hope in
the LORD.

Psalm 31:24

Happy is he that hath the God of Jacob for
his help, whose hope is in the LORD his God:
Which made heaven, and earth, the sea, and
all that therein is: which keepeth truth
for ever.

Psalm 146:5–6

Hope maketh not ashamed; because the love
of God is shed abroad in our hearts by the
Holy Ghost which is given unto us.

Romans 5:5

Behold, the eye of the LORD is upon them
that fear him, upon them that hope in
his mercy.

Psalm 33:18

HOSPITALITY

Jesus said, "Whosoever shall give you a cup of water to drink in my name, because ye belong to Christ, verily I say unto you, he shall not lose his reward."

Mark 9:41

Be not forgetful to entertain strangers: for thereby some have entertained angels unawares.

Hebrews 13:2

He that hath a bountiful eye shall be blessed; for he giveth of his bread to the poor.

Proverbs 22:9

A good man showeth favour, and lendeth: he will guide his affairs with discretion. Surely he shall not be moved for ever: the righteous shall be in everlasting remembrance.

Psalm 112:5–6

Is not this the fast that I have chosen?... Is it to deal thy bread to the hungry, and that thou bring the poor that are cast out to thy house? when thou seest the naked, that thou cover him; and that thou hide not thyself from thine own flesh? Then shall thy light break forth as the morning, and thine health shall spring forth speedily: and thy righteousness shall go before thee; and the glory of the LORD shall be thy rearward.

Isaiah 58:6–8

Jesus said, "He that receiveth you receiveth me, and he that receiveth me receiveth him that sent me. He that receiveth a prophet in the name of a prophet shall receive a prophet's reward; and he that receiveth a righteous man in the name of a righteous man shall receive a righteous man's reward. And whosoever shall give to drink unto one of these little ones a cup of cold water only in the name of a disciple, verily I say unto you, he shall in no wise lose his reward."

Matthew 10:40–42

HUMILITY

Jesus called a little child unto him, and set him in the midst of them,... [and] said, "Whosoever therefore shall humble himself as this little child, the same is greatest in the kingdom of heaven."

Matthew 18:2, 4

God resisteth the proud, but giveth grace unto the humble.... Humble yourselves in the sight of the Lord, and he shall lift you up.

James 4:6, 10

By humility and the fear of the LORD are riches, and honour, and life.

Proverbs 22:4

The fear of the LORD is the instruction of wisdom; and before honour is humility.

Proverbs 15:33

A man's pride shall bring him low: but
honour shall uphold the humble in spirit.

Proverbs 29:23

The meek will God guide in judgment: and
the meek will he teach his way.

Psalm 25:9

Great is our LORD, and of great power: his
understanding is infinite. The LORD lifteth
up the meek.

Psalm 147:5–6

All of you be subject one to another, and be
clothed with humility: for God resiseth the
proud, and giveth grace to the humble.
Humble yourselves therefore under the
mighty hand of God, that he may exalt you in
due time.

1 Peter 5:5–6

INTEGRITY

The integrity of the upright shall guide them.

Proverbs 11:3

As for me, thou upholdest me in mine integrity, and settest me before thy face for ever, O Lord.

Psalm 41:12

I know … my God, that thou triest the heart, and hast pleasure in uprightness.

1 Chronicles 29:17

The LORD God is a sun and shield: the LORD will give grace and glory: no good thing will he withhold from them that walk uprightly.

Psalm 84:11

Jesus said, "He that is faithful in that which is least is faithful also in much."

Luke 16:10

The LORD layeth up sound wisdom for the righteous: he is a buckler to them that walk uprightly.

Proverbs 2:7

O keep my soul, and deliver me: let me not be ashamed; for I put my trust in thee. Let integrity and uprightness preserve me; for I wait on thee, O Lord.

Psalm 25:20—21

The just man walketh in his integrity, his children are blessed after him.

Proverbs 20:7

Judge me, O LORD; for I have walked in mine integrity: I have trusted also in the LORD; therefore I shall not slide.

Psalm 26:1

The LORD shall judge the people: judge me,
O LORD, according to my righteousness, and
according to mine integrity that is in me. Oh
let the wickedness of the wicked come to an
end; but establish the just: for the righteous
God trieth the hearts and reins. My defence
is of God, which saveth the upright in heart.

Psalm 7:8–10

The mouth of the just bringeth forth wisdom.

Proverbs 10:31

Behold, thou desirest truth in the inward
parts, O God: and in the hidden part thou
shalt make me to know wisdom.

Psalm 51:6

The LORD is nigh unto all them that call
upon him, to all that call upon him in truth.

Psalm 145:18

INTERCESSION

The Spirit ... helpeth our infirmities: for we know not what we should pray for as we ought: but the Spirit itself maketh intercession for us with groanings which cannot be uttered. And he that searcheth the hearts knoweth what is the mind of the Spirit, because he maketh intercession for the saints according to the will of God.

Romans 8:26—27

Jesus is able also to save them to the uttermost that come unto God by him, seeing he ever liveth to make intercession for them.

Hebrews 7:25

"If my people, which are called by my name, shall humble themselves, and pray, and seek my face, and turn from their wicked ways; then will I hear form heaven, and will forgive their sin, and will heal their land," saith the Lord.

2 Chronicles 7:14

The Messiah hath poured out his soul unto
death: and he was numbered with the
transgressors; and he bare the sin of many,
and made intercession for the transgressors.

Isaiah 53:12

God saw that there was no man, and
wondered that there was no intercessor:
therefore his arm brought salvation unto
him; and his righteousness, it sustained
him.... So shall they fear the name of the
LORD from the west, and his glory from the
rising of the sun. When the enemy shall
come in like a flood, the Spirit of the LORD
shall lift up a standard against him.

Isaiah 59:16, 19

Who shall lay any thing to the charge of
God's elect? It is God that justifieth. Who is
he that condemneth? It is Christ that died,
yea rather, that is risen again, who is even at
the right hand of God, who also maketh
intercession for us.

Romans 8:33–34

JOY

They that sow in tears shall reap in joy. He that goeth forth and weepeth, bearing precious seed, shall doubtless come again with rejoicing, bringing his sheaves with him.

Psalm 126:5—6

Thou wilt show me the path of life, O Lord: in thy presence is fulness of joy; at thy right hand there are pleasures for evermore.

Psalm 16:11

Light is sown for the righteous, and gladness for the upright in heart.

Psalm 97:11

Thou hast loved righteousness, and hated iniquity; therefore God, even thy God, hath anointed thee with the oil of gladness above thy fellows.

Hebrews 1:9

A man hath joy by the answer of his mouth:
and a word spoken in due season, how good
is it!

Proverbs 15:23

I will greatly rejoice in the LORD, my soul
shall be joyful in my God; for he hath clothed
me with the garments of salvation, he hath
covered me with the robe of righteousness.

Isaiah 61:10

The LORD thy God shall bless thee in all
thine increase, and in all the works of thine
hands, therefore thou shalt surely rejoice.

Deuteronomy 16:15

Jesus said, "Hitherto have ye asked nothing
in my name: ask, and ye shall receive, that
your joy may be full."

John 16:24

JUSTICE

He is the Rock, his work is perfect: for all his ways are judgment: a God of truth and without iniquity, just and right is he.

Deuteronomy 32:4

That which is altogether just shalt thou follow, that thou mayest live, and inherit the land which the LORD thy God giveth thee.

Deuteronomy 16:20

Dearly beloved, avenge not yourselves, but rather give place unto wrath: for it is written, Vengeance is mine; I will repay, saith the Lord.

Romans 12:19

The LORD executeth righteousness and judgment for all that are oppressed.

Psalm 103:6

O let the nations be glad and sing for joy: for thou shalt judge the people righteously, and govern the nations upon earth, O God.

Psalm 67:4

Not the hearers of the law are just before God, but the doers of the law shall be justified.

Romans 2:13

The LORD loveth judgment, and forsaketh not his saints; they are preserved for ever.

Psalm 37:28

Therefore will the LORD wait, that he may be gracious unto you, and therefore will he be exalted, that he may have mercy upon you: for the LORD is a God of judgment: blessed are all they that wait for him.

Isaiah 30:18

The righteous LORD loveth righteousness; his countenance doth behold the upright.

Psalm 11:7

We ourselves glory in you in the churches of God for your patience and faith in all your persecutions and tribulations that ye endure: Which is a manifest token of the righteous judgment of God, that ye may be counted worthy of the kingdom of God, for which ye also suffer: Seeing it is a righteous thing with God to recompense tribulation to them that trouble you; and to you who are troubled rest with us, when the Lord Jesus shall be revealed with his mighty angels.

2 Thessalonians 1:4–7

All have sinned, and come short of the glory
of God; Being justified freely by his grace
through the redemption that is in Christ
Jesus: Whom God hath set forth to be a
propitiation through faith in his blood, to
declare his righteousness for the remission of
sins that are past, through the forbearance of
God; To declare, I say, at this time his
righteousness that he might be just, and the
justifier of him which believeth in Jesus.

Romans 3:23–26

God hath given meat unto them that fear
him: he will ever be mindful of his covenant.
He hath shown his people the power of his
works, that he may give them the heritage of
the heathen. The works of his hands are
verity and judgment; all his commandments
are sure. They stand fast for ever and ever,
and are done in truth and uprightness.

Psalm 111:5–8

KINDNESS

The desire of a man is his kindness.

Proverbs 19:22

O praise the LORD, all ye nations: praise him,
all ye people. For his merciful kindness is
great toward us: and the truth of the LORD
endureth for ever. Praise ye the LORD.

Psalm 117:1–2

Who can find a virtuous woman: for her
price is far above rubies. ... She openeth her
mouth with wisdom; and in her tongue is the
law of kindness.

Proverbs 31:10, 26

He that hath pity upon the poor lendeth
unto the LORD; and that which he hath given
will he pay him again.

Proverbs 19:17

Let him that glorieth glory in this, that he understandeth and knoweth me, that I am the LORD which exercise lovingkindness, judgment, and righteousness, in the earth: for in these things I delight, saith the LORD.

Jeremiah 9:24

Blessed be the LORD: for he hath shown me his marvelous kindness in a strong city.

Psalm 31:21

Let, I pray thee, O Lord, thy merciful kindness be for my comfort, according to thy word unto thy servant. Let thy tender mercies come unto me, that I may live: for thy law is my delight.

Psalm 119:76–77

KINGDOM OF GOD

Jesus said, "Take no thought, saying, What shall we eat? or, What shall we drink? or, Wherewithal shall we be clothed?... for your heavenly Father knoweth that ye have need of all these things. But seek ye first the kingdom of God, and his righteousness; and all these things shall be added unto you."

Matthew 6:31–33

Wherefore we receiving a kingdom which cannot be moved, let us have grace, whereby we may serve God acceptably with reverence and godly fear.

Hebrews 12:28

Jesus said, "Rejoice not, that the spirits are subject unto you; but rather rejoice, because your names are written in heaven."

Luke 10:20

Let not then your good be evil spoken of: For the kingdom of God is not meat and drink; but righteousness, and peace, and joy in the Holy Ghost. For he that in these things serveth Christ is acceptable to God, and approved of men.

Romans 14:16—18

Jesus said, "Fear not, little flock; for it is your Father's good pleasure to give you the kingdom."

Luke 12:32

Jesus said, "Verily I say unto you, There is no man that hath left house, or parents, or brethren, or wife, or children, for the kingdom of God's sake, Who shall not receive manifold more in this present time, and in the world to come life everlasting."

Luke 18:29—30

[Give] thanks unto the Father, which hath
made us meet to be partakers of the
inheritance of the saints in light: Who hath
delivered us from the power of darkness, and
hath translated us into the kingdom of his dear
Son: In whom we have redemption through
his blood, even the forgiveness of sins.

Colossians 1:12–14

Brethren, give diligence to make your calling
and election sure: for if ye do these things, ye
shall never fall: For so an entrance shall be
ministered unto you abundantly into the
everlasting kingdom of our Lord and Saviour
Jesus Christ.

2 Peter 1:10–11

Hearken my beloved brethren, Hath not
God chosen the poor of this world rich in
faith, and heirs of the kingdom which he
hath promised to them that love him?

James 2:5

LEADERSHIP

Jesus is the head of the body, the church:
who is the beginning, the firstborn from
the dead; that in all things he might have
the preeminence.

Colossians 1:18

Obey them that have the rule over you, and
submit yourselves: for they watch for your
souls, as they that must give account, that
they may do it with joy, and not with grief:
for that is unprofitable for you.

Hebrews 13:17

Submit yourself to every ordinance of man for
the Lord's sake: whether it be to the king, as
supreme; Or unto governors, as unto them that
are sent by him for the punishment of evildoers,
and for the praise of them that do well.

1 Peter 2:13—14

Ye younger, submit yourselves unto the elder.
Yea, all of you be subject one to another, and
be clothed with humility: for God resisteth
the proud, and giveth grace to the humble.

1 Peter 5:5

LIFE

Jesus said, "I am the bread of life: he that cometh to me shall never hunger; and he that believeth on me shall never thirst."

John 6:25

The LORD is my light and my salvation; whom shall I fear? the LORD is the strength of my life; of whom shall I be afraid?

Psalm 27:1

There is therefore now no condemnation to them which are in Christ Jesus, who walk not after the flesh, but after the Spirit. For the law of the Spirit of life in Christ Jesus hath made me free from the law of sin and death.

Romans 8:1—2

If the Spirit of him that raised up Jesus from the dead dwell in you, he that raised up Christ from the dead shall also quicken your mortal bodies by his Spirit that dwelleth in you. Therefore, brethren, we are debtors, not to the flesh, to live after the flesh. For if ye live after the flesh, ye shall die: but if ye through the Spirit do mortify the deeds of the body, ye shall live.

Romans 8:11–13

When we were enemies, we were reconciled to God by the death of his Son, much more, being reconciled, we shall be saved by his life.

Romans 5:10

If by one man's offence death reigned by one; much more they which receive abundance of grace and of the gift of righteousness shall reign in life by one, Jesus Christ.

Romans 5:17

Set your affection on things above, not on things on the earth. For ye are dead, and your life is hid with Christ in God. When Christ, who is our life, shall appear, then shall ye also appear with him in glory.

Colossians 3:2—4

Bodily exercise profiteth little: but godliness is profitable unto all things, having promise of the life that now is, and of that which is to come.

1 Timothy 4:8

The mouth of a righteous man is a well of life.

Proverbs 10:11

Jesus said, "I am the resurrection, and the life: he that believeth in me, though he were dead, yet shall he live: And whosoever liveth and believeth in me shall never die."

John 11:25—26

With thee is the fountain of life, O Lord: in thy light shall we see light.

Psalm 36:9

Thou wilt show me the path of life: in thy presence is fullness of joy; at thy right hand there are pleasures for evermore, O Lord.

Psalm 16:11

LONELINESS

"Behold, I am with thee, and will keep thee
in all places whither thou goest, and will
bring thee again into this land; for I will not
leave thee, until I have done that which I
have spoken to thee of," saith the Lord.

Genesis 28:15

When my father and my mother forsake me,
then the LORD will take me up.

Psalm 27:10

A father of the fatherless, and a judge of the
widows, is God in his holy habitation.
God setteth the solitary in families.

Psalm 68:5—6

Jesus spake, saying, "Lo, I am with you
always, even unto the end of the world."

Matthew 28:20

I am continually with thee: thou hast holden
me by my right hand, O Lord.

Psalm 73:23

The LORD redeemeth the soul of his servants: and none of them that trust in him shall be desolate.

Psalm 34:22

Know ye that the LORD he is God: it is he that hath made us, and not we ourselves; we are his people, and the sheep of his pasture.

Psalm 100:3

Jesus said, "Behold, I stand at the door, and knock: if any man hear my voice, and open the door, I will come in to him, and will sup with him, and he with me."

Revelation 3:20

Jesus said, "Ye are my friends, if ye do whatsoever I command you. Henceforth I call you not servants; for the servant knoweth not what his lord doeth: but I have called you friends; for all things that I have heard of my Father I have made known unto you."

John 15:14–15

Jesus said, "I will not leave you comfortless: I will come to you."

John 14:18

The LORD is good unto them that wait for him, to the soul that seeketh him.

Lamentations 3:25

The LORD preserveth the strangers; he relieveth the fatherless and widow.

Psalm 146:9

I will receive you, and will be a Father unto you, And ye shall be my sons and daughters, saith the Lord Almighty.

2 Corinthians 6:17–18

Draw nigh to God, and he will draw nigh to you.

James 4:8

A man that hath friends must show himself
friendly: and there is a friend that sticketh
closer than a brother.

Proverbs 18:24

The LORD saith, "I will betroth thee unto me
for ever; yea, I will betroth thee unto me in
righteousness, and in judgment, and in
lovingkindness, and in mercies. I will even
betroth thee unto me in faithfulness: and
thou shalt know the LORD."

Hosea 2:19—20

God hath said, "I will never leave thee, nor
forsake thee."

Hebrews 13:5

LOVE

Put on therefore, as the elect of God, holy
and beloved, bowels of mercies, kindness,
humbleness of mind, meekness,
longsuffering. ... Above all these things put
on charity, which is the bond of perfectness.

Colossians 3:14

Abideth faith, hope, charity, these three; but
the greatest of these is charity.

1 Corinthians 13:13

Charity suffereth long, and is kind; charity
envieth not; charity vaunteth not itself, is not
puffed up, Doth not behave itself unseemly,
seeketh not her own, is not easily provoked,
thinketh no evil; Rejoiceth not in iniquity,
but rejoiceth in the truth; Beareth all things,
believeth all things, hopeth all things,
endureth all things. Charity never faileth.

1 Corinthians 13:4–8

I am persuaded, that neither death, nor life,
nor angels, nor principalities, nor powers, nor
things present, nor things to come, nor
height, nor depth, nor any other creature,
shall be able to separate us from the love of
God, which is in Christ Jesus our Lord.

Romans 8:38–39

Jesus said, "He that hath my commandments,
and keepeth them, he it is that loveth me:
and he that loveth me shall be loved of my
Father, and I will love him, and will manifest
myself to him."

John 14:21

If we love one another, God dwelleth in us,
and his love is perfected in us.

1 John 4:12

Beloved, let us love one another: for love is of God; and every one that loveth is born of God, and knoweth God.

1 John 4:7

Jesus said, "If a man love me, he will keep my words: and my Father will love him, and we will come unto him, and make our abode with him."

John 14:23

Jesus said, "I say unto you, Love your enemies, bless them that curse you, do good to them that hate you, and pray for them which despitefully use you, and persecute you; That ye may be the children of your Father which is in heaven."

Matthew 5:44–45

God who is rich in mercy, for his great love
wherewith he loved us, Even when we were
dead in sins hath quickened us together with
Christ, (by grace ye are saved;) And hath
raised us up together, and made us sit
together in heavenly places in Christ Jesus.

Ephesians 2:4–6

The LORD hath appeared of old unto me,
saying, Yea, I have loved thee with an
everlasting love: therefore with
lovingkindness have I drawn thee.

Jeremiah 31:3

The LORD openeth the eyes of the blind: the
LORD raiseth them that are bowed down: the
LORD loveth the righteous: The LORD
preserveth the strangers; he relieveth the
fatherless and widow.

Psalm 146:8–9

Hear me speedily, O LORD.... Cause me to hear thy lovingkindness in the morning; for in thee do I trust.

Psalm 143:7–8

He that covereth a transgression seeketh love.

Proverbs 17:9

There is no fear in love; but perfect love casteth out fear.

1 John 4:18

MEDITATION

This book of the law shall not depart out of thy mouth; but thou shalt meditate therein day and night, that thou mayest observe to do according to all that is written therein: for then thou shalt make thy way prosperous, and then thou shalt have good success.

Joshua 1:8

Blessed is the man that walketh not in the counsel of the ungodly, nor standeth in the way of sinners, nor sitteth in the seat of the scornful. But his delight is in the law of the LORD; and in his law doth he meditate day and night. And he shall be like a tree planted by the rivers of water, that bringeth forth his fruit in his season; his leaf also shall not wither; and whatsoever he doeth shall prosper.

Psalm 1:1–3

I will sing unto the LORD as long as I live: I will sing praise to my God while I have my being. My meditation of him shall be sweet: I will be glad in the LORD.

Psalm 104:33—34

O how love I thy law! It is my meditation all the day. Thou through thy commandments hast made me wiser than mine enemies: for they are ever with me. I have more understanding than all my teahers: for thy testimonies are my meditation.

Psalm 119:97—99

MERCY

The mercy of the LORD is from everlasting to everlasting upon them that fear him, and his righteousness unto children's children.

Psalm 103:17

Blessed are the merciful: for they shall obtain mercy.

Matthew 5:7

Thou, LORD, art good, and ready to forgive; and plenteous in mercy unto all them that call upon thee.

Psalm 86:5

God's mercy is on them that fear him from generation to generation.

Luke 1:50

Let the wicked forsake his way, and the unrighteous man his thoughts: and let him return unto the LORD, and he will have mercy upon him; and to our God, for he will abundantly pardon.

Isaiah 55:7

Blessed be the God and Father of our Lord Jesus Christ, which according to his abundant mercy hath begotten us again unto a lively hope by the resurrection of Jesus Christ from the dead.

1 Peter 1:3

All the paths of the LORD are mercy and truth unto such as keep his covenant and his testimonies.

Psalm 25:10

MINISTRY

The King [shall] say unto them on his right
hand, Come, ye blessed of my Father, inherit
the kingdom prepared for you from the
foundation of the world: For I was an
hungered, and ye gave me meat: I was thirsty,
and ye gave me drink: I was a stranger, and ye
took me in: Naked, and ye clothed me: I was
sick, and ye visited me: I was in prison, and
ye came unto me.

Then shall the righteous answer him, saying,
Lord, when saw we thee an hungered, and
fed thee? or thirsty, and gave thee drink?
When saw we thee a stranger, and took thee
in? or naked, and clothed thee? Or when saw
we thee sick, or in prison, and came unto
thee?

And the King shall answer and say unto
them, Verily I say unto you, Inasmuch as ye
have done it unto one of the least of these my
brethren, ye have done it unto me.

Matthew 25:34–40

Jesus said, "When thou makest a dinner or a
supper, call not thy friends, nor thy brethren,
neither thy kinsmen, nor thy rich neighbours;
lest they also bid thee again, and a
recompence be made thee. But when thou
makest a feast, call the poor, the maimed, the
lame, the blind: And thou shalt be blessed;
for they cannot recompense thee: for thou
shalt be recompensed at the resurrection of
the just."

Luke 14:12–14

If any man be in Christ, he is a new creature:
old things are passed away; behold, all things
are become new. And all things are of God,
who hath reconciled us to himself by Jesus
Christ, and hath given to us the ministry of
reconciliation.

2 Corinthians 5:17–18

God gave some, apostles; and some, prophets; and some, evangelists; and some, pastors and teachers; For the perfecting of the saints, for the work of the ministry, for the edifying of the body of Christ: Till we all come in the unity of the faith, and of the knowledge of the Son of God, unto a perfect man, unto the measure of the stature of the fulness of Christ.

Ephesians 4:11–13

MONEY

Honour the LORD with thy substance, and
with the firstfruits of all thine increase: So
shall thy barns be filled with plenty, and thy
presses shall burst out with new wine.

Proverbs 3:9–10

Jesus said, "When thou doest thine alms, do
not sound a trumpet before thee, as the
hypocrites do in the synagogues and in the
streets, that they may have glory of men.
Verily I say unto you, They have their
reward. But when thou doest alms, let not
thy left hand know what thy right hand
doeth: That thine alms may be in secret: and
thy Father which seeth in secret himself shall
reward thee openly.

Matthew 6:2–4

A good man leaveth an inheritance to his children's children: and the wealth of the sinner is laid up for the just.

Proverbs 13:22

Render therefore to all their dues: tribute to whom tribute is due; custom to whom custom; fear to whom fear; honour to whom honour. Owe no man any thing, but to love one another: for he that loveth another hath fulfilled the law.

Romans 13:7–8

Wisdom is a defence, and money is a defence: but the excellency of knowledge is, that wisdom giveth life to them that have it.

Ecclesiastes 7:12

[Jesus told this parable]: A certain nobleman went into a far country to receive for himself a kingdom, and to return. And he called his ten servants, and delivered them ten pounds, and said unto them, Occupy till I come.... And it came to pass, that when he was returned, having received the kingdom, then he commanded these servants to be called unto him, to whom he had given the money, that he might know how much every man had gained by trading. Then came the first, saying, Lord, thy pound hath gained ten pounds. And he said unto him, Well, thou good servant: because thou hast been faithful in a very little, have thou authority over ten cities. And the second came, saying, Lord, thy pound hath gained five pounds. And he said likewise to him, Be thou also over five cities. ... For I say unto you, That unto every one which hath shall be given.

Luke 19:12—13, 15—19, 26

OBEDIENCE

He that doeth the will of God abideth for ever.

1 John 2:17

Jesus said, "Whosoever heareth these sayings of mine, and doeth them, I will liken him unto a wise man, which built his house upon a rock: And the rain descended, and the floods came, and the winds blew, and beat upon that house; and it fell not: for it was founded upon a rock."

Matthew 7:24—25

Whoso looketh into the perfect law of liberty, and continueth therein, he being not a forgetful hearer, but a doer of the work, this man shall be blessed in his deed.

James 1:25

Jesus said, "For verily I say unto you, Till heaven and earth pass, one jot or one tittle shall in no wise pass from the law, till all be fulfilled. Whosoever therefore shall break one of these least commandments, and shall teach men so, he shall be called the least in the kingdom of heaven: but whosoever shall do and teach them, the same shall be called great in the kingdom of heaven."

Matthew 5:19

Jesus said, "If ye keep my commandments, ye shall abide in my love."

John 15:10

As by one man's disobedience many were made sinners, so by the obedience of one shall many be made righteous.

Romans 5:19

PAIN

God shall wipe away all tears from their eyes;
and there shall be no more death, neither
sorrow, nor crying, neither shall there be any
more pain: for the former things are passed
away.

Revelation 21:4

No chastening for the present seemeth to be
joyous, but grievous: nevertheless afterward it
yieldeth the peaceable fruit of righteousness
unto them which are exercised thereby.

Hebrews 12:11

Heal me, O LORD, and I shall be healed; save
me, and I shall be saved: for thou art my
praise.

Jeremiah 17:14

Look upon mine affliction and my pain; and
forgive all my sins, O Lord.

Psalm 25:18

A great multitude, which no man could number, of all nations, and kindreds, and people, and tongues, stood before the throne, and before the Lamb, clothed with white robes, and palms in their hands.... These are they which came out of great tribulation, and have washed their robes, and made them white in the blood of the Lamb.... The Lamb which is in the midst of the throne shall feed them, and shall lead them unto living fountains of waters: and God shall wipe away all tears from their eyes.

Revelation 7:9, 14, 17

"Behold, I will bring [my people] health and cure, and I will cure them, and will reveal unto them the abundance of peace and truth," saith the Lord.

Jeremiah 33:6

PARENTING

Correct thy son, and he shall give thee rest;
yea, he shall give delight unto thy soul.

Proverbs 29:17

Thou shalt keep ... God's statutes, and his
commandments, ... that it may go well with
thee, and with thy children after thee, and
that thou mayest prolong thy days upon the
earth, which the LORD thy God giveth thee,
for ever.

Deuteronomy 4:40

Children's children are the crown of old men;
and the glory of children are their fathers.

Proverbs 17:6

All thy children shall be taught of the LORD;
and great shall be the peace of thy children.

Isaiah 54:13

The living, the living, he shall praise thee,
Lord, as I do this day: the father to the
children shall make known thy truth.

Isaiah 38:19

Train up a child in the way he should go: and
when he is old, he will not depart from it.

Proverbs 22:6

The LORD thy God will make thee plenteous
in every work of thine hand, in the fruit of
thy body, ... and in the fruit of thy land, for
good: for the LORD will again rejoice over
thee for good, as he rejoiced over thy fathers.

Deuteronomy 30:9

PATIENCE

My brethren, count it all joy when ye fall into divers temptations; Knowing this, that the trying of your faith worketh patience.

James 1:2–3

Cast not away ... your confidence, which hath great recompense of reward. For ye have need of patience, that, after ye have done the will of God, ye might receive the promise.

Hebrews 10:35–36

Seeing we also are compassed about with so great a cloud of witnesses, let us lay aside every weight, and the sin which doth so easily beset us, and let us run with patience the race that is set before us, Looking unto Jesus the author and finisher of our faith.

Hebrews 12:1–2

I waited patiently for the LORD; and he
inclined unto me, and heard my cry.

Psalm 40:1

He that is slow to wrath is of great
understanding: but he that is hasty of spirit
exalteth folly.

Proverbs 14:29

Let patience have her perfect work, that ye
may be perfect and entire, wanting nothing.

James 1:4

PEACE

Mark the perfect man, and behold the upright: for the end of that man is peace.

Psalm 37:37

Be careful for nothing; but in every thing by prayer and supplication with thanksgiving let your requests be made known unto God. The peace of God, which passeth all understanding, shall keep your hearts and minds through Christ Jesus.

Philippians 4:6–7

Thou wilt keep him in perfect peace, whose mind is stayed on thee: because he trusteth in thee, O Lord.

Isaiah 26:3

Being justified by faith, we have peace with God through our Lord Jesus Christ: By whom also we have access by faith into this grace wherein we stand, and rejoice in hope of the glory of God.

Romans 5:1–2

Jesus said, "Blessed are the peacemakers: for they shall be called the children of God."

Matthew 5:9

Jesus said, "Peace I leave with you, my peace I give unto you: not as the world giveth, give I unto you. Let not your heart be troubled, neither let it be afraid."

John 14:27

Be perfect, be of good comfort, be of one mind, live in peace; and the God of love and peace shall be with you.

2 Corinthians 13:11

Great peace have they which love thy law, O Lord.

Psalm 119:165

To be carnally minded is death; but to be spiritually minded is life and peace.

Romans 8:6

The fruit of righteousness is sown in peace of them that make peace.

James 3:18

Glory, honour, and peace, to every man that worketh good, to the Jew first, and also to the Gentile; For there is no respect of persons with God.

Romans 2:10–11

How beautiful are the feet of them that preach the gospel of peace, and bring glad tidings of good things!

Romans 10:15

The kingdom of God is not meat and drink; but righteousness, and peace, and joy in the Holy Ghost. For he that in these things serveth Christ is acceptable to God, and approved of men. Let us therefore follow after the things which make for peace, and things wherewith one may edify another.

Romans 14:17–19

The God of hope fill you with all joy and peace in believing, that ye may abound in hope, through the power of the Holy Ghost.

Romans 15:13

The God of peace shall bruise Satan under your feet shortly. The grace of our Lord Jesus Christ be with you.

Romans 16:20

God is not the author of confusion, but of peace.

1 Corinthians 14:33

When a man's ways please the LORD, he maketh even his enemies to be at peace with him.

Proverbs 16:7

Let the peace of God rule in your hearts, to the which also ye are called in one body; and be ye thankful.

Colossians 3:15

PERSEVERANCE

Blessed is the man that endureth temptation:
for when he is tried, he shall receive the
crown of life, which the Lord hath promised
to them that love him.

James 1:12

To them who by patient continuance in well
doing seek for glory and honour and
immortality, eternal life.

Romans 2:7

Let us not be weary in well doing: for in due
season we shall reap, if we faint not.

Galatians 6:9

The God of all grace, who hath called us unto
his eternal glory by Christ Jesus, after that ye
have suffered a while, make you perfect,
stablish, strengthen, settle you.

1 Peter 5:10

Our light affliction, which is but for a moment, worketh for us a far more exceeding and eternal weight of glory, While we look not at the things which are seen, but at the things which are not seen: for the things which are seen are temporal; but the things which are not seen are eternal.

2 Corinthians 4:17–18

The Lord direct your hearts into the love of God, and into the patient waiting for Christ.

2 Thessalonians 3:5

POWER

The God of Israel is he that giveth strength
and power unto his people.

Psalm 68:35

When I am old and grayheaded, O God,
forsake me not; until I have shown thy
strength unto this generation, and thy power
to every one that is to come.

Psalm 71:18

The LORD is good to all: and his tender
mercies are over all his works. All thy works
shall praise thee, O LORD; and thy saints
shall bless thee. They shall speak of the glory
of thy kingdom, and talk of thy power.

Psalm 145:9—11

God has shown his people the power of
his works.

Psalm 111:6

Great is our Lord, and of great power: his understanding is infinite. The LORD lifteth up the meek.

Psalm 147:5–6

Hast thou not known? hast thou not heard, that the everlasting God, the LORD, the Creator of the ends of the earth, fainteth not, neither is weary? there is no searching of his understanding. He giveth power to the faint; and to them that have no might he increaseth strength.

Isaiah 40:28–29

Not by might, nor by power, but by my spirit, saith the LORD of hosts.

Zechariah 4:6

Jesus said, "Behold, I give unto you power to tread on serpents and scorpions, and over all the power of the enemy: and nothing shall by any means hurt you."

Luke 10:19

As many as received Jesus, to them gave he power to become the sons of God, even to them that believe on his name.

John 1:12

I am not ashamed of the gospel of Christ: for it is the power of God unto salvation to every one that believeth.

Romans 1:16

The preaching of the cross is to them that perish foolishness; but unto us which are saved it is the power of God.

1 Corinthians 1:18

The kingdom of God is not in word, but in power.

1 Corinthians 4:20

Unto him that is able to do exceeding abundantly above all that we ask or think, according to the power that worketh in us. Unto him be glory in the church by Christ Jesus throughout all ages, world without end.

Ephesians 3:20–21

PRAISE

O come, let us worship and bow down: let us kneel before the LORD our maker. For he is our God; and we are the people of his pasture, and the sheep of his hand.

Psalm 95:6

Praise the LORD with harp: sing unto him with the psaltery and an instrument of ten strings. Sing unto him a new song; play skillfully with a loud noise. For the word of the LORD is right; and all his works are done in truth.

Psalm 33:2—4

Thou art holy, O thou that inhabitest the praises of Israel. Our fathers trusted in thee: they trusted, and thou didst deliver them.

Psalm 22:3—4

Ye are a chosen generation, a royal priesthood, an holy nation, a peculiar people; that ye should show forth the praises of God who hath called you out of darkness into his marvellous light.

1 Peter 2:9

Let the saints be joyful in glory: let them sing aloud upon their beds. Let the high praises of God be in their mouth.

Psalm 149:5—6

Rejoice in the LORD, O ye righteous: for praise is comely for the upright.

Psalm 33: 1

Praise ye the LORD. Sing unto the LORD a
new song, and his praise in the congregation
of saints. Let Israel rejoice in him that made
him: let the children of Zion be joyful in
their King.

Psalm 149:1–2

I will mention the lovingkindnesses of the
LORD, and the praises of the LORD,
according to all that the LORD hath bestowed
on us, and the great goodness toward the
house of Israel, which he hath bestowed on
them according to his mercies, and according
to the multitude of his lovingkindnesses. For
he said, Surely they are my people, children
that will not lie: so he was their Savior.

Isaiah 63:7–8

I will praise thee, O LORD, with my
whole heart; I will show forth all thy
marvellous works.

Psalm 9:1

A voice came out of the throne, saying, Praise our God, all ye his servants, and ye that fear him, both small and great. And I heard as it were the voice of a great multitude, and as the voice of many waters, and as the voice of mighty thunderings, saying, Alleluia: for the Lord God omnipotent reigneth.

Revelation 19:5-6

I will extol thee, O LORD; for thou hast lifted me up, and hast not made my foes to rejoice over me. O LORD my God, I cried unto thee, and thou hast healed me.

Psalm 30:1–2

PRAYER

The prayer of faith shall save the sick, and
the Lord shall raise him up; and if he have
committed sins, they shall be forgiven him.

James 5:15

The eyes of the Lord are over the righteous,
and his ears are open unto their prayers.

1 Peter 3:12

Confess your faults one to another, and pray
one for another, that ye may be healed.

James 5:16

The LORD is far from the wicked: but he
heareth the prayer of the righteous.

Proverbs 15:29

Jesus said, "All things, whatsoever ye shall ask in prayer, believing, ye shall receive."

Matthew 21:21–22

"If my people, which are called by my name, shall humble themselves, and pray, and seek my face, and turn from their wicked ways; then will I hear from heaven, and will forgive their sin, and will heal their land," saith the Lord.

2 Chronicles 7:14

"Shall ye call upon me, and ye shall go and pray unto me, and I will hearken unto you," saith the Lord.

Jeremiah 29:12

The prayer of the upright is God's delight.

Proverbs 15:8

Hearken unto the voice of my cry, my King, and my God: for unto thee will I pray. My voice shalt thou hear in the morning, O LORD; in the morning will I direct my prayer unto thee, and will look up.

Psalm 5:2–3

Jesus said, "Therefore I say unto you, What things soever ye desire, when ye pray, believe that ye receive them, and ye shall have them."

Mark 11:24

As for me, I shall call upon God; and the LORD shall save me. Evening, and morning, and at noon, will I pray, and cry aloud: and he shall hear my voice.

Psalm 55:16–17

Shall everyone that is godly pray unto thee, Lord, in a time when thou mayest be found: surely in the floods of great waters they shall not come nigh unto him.

Psalm 32:6

PRIDE

Jesus said, "Every one that exalteth himself shall be abased; and he that humbleth himself shall be exalted."

Luke 18:14

A man's pride shall bring him low: but honour shall uphold the humble in spirit.

Proverbs 29:23

The LORD taketh pleasure in his people: he will beautify the meek with salvation.

Psalm 149:4

The fear of the LORD is the instruction of wisdom; and before honour is humility.

Proverbs 15:33

The LORD lifteth up the meek: he casteth the wicked down to the ground.

Psalm 147:6

The meek will God guide in judgment: and the meek will he teach his way.

Psalm 25:9

Better is it to be of an humble spirit with the lowly, than to divide the spoil with the proud.

Proverbs 16:19

PRIORITIES

Said Jesus unto his disciples, "If any man will come after me, let him deny himself, and take up his cross, and follow me. For whosoever will save his life shall lose it: and whosoever will lose his life for my sake shall find it."

Matthew 16:24–25

He that followeth after righteousness and mercy findeth life, righteousness, and honour.

Proverbs 21:21

Children, obey your parents in the Lord: for this is right. Honor your father and mother; which is the first commandment with promise; that it may be well with thee, and thou mayest live long on the earth.

Ephesians 6:1–3

Delight thyself also in the LORD; and he shall give thee the desires of thine heart. Commit thy way unto the LORD; trust also in him; and he shall bring it to pass.

Psalm 37:4–5

Be obedient to them that are your masters
according to the flesh, with fear and
trembling, in singleness of your heart, as to
Christ; Not with eyeservice, as menpleasers;
but as the servants of Christ, doing the will of
God from the heart; With good will doing
service, as to the Lord, and not to men:
Knowing that whatsoever good thing any man
doeth, the same shall he receive of the Lord.

Ephesians 6:5–8

This one thing I do, forgetting those things which
are behind, and reaching forth unto those things
which are before, I press toward the mark for the
prize of the high calling of God in Christ Jesus.

Philippians 3:13–14

If ye ... be risen with Christ, seek those things
which are above, where Christ sitteth on the
right hand of God. Set your affection on things
above, not on things on the earth. For ye are
dead, and your life is hid with Christ in God.
When Christ, who is our life, shall appear, then
shall ye also appear with him in glory.

Colossians 3:1–4

PROPHECY

It shall come to pass in the last days, saith
God, I will pour out of my Spirit upon all
flesh: and your sons and your daughters shall
prophesy, and your young men shall see
visions, and your old men shall
dream dreams.

Acts 2:17

We have also a more sure word of prophecy;
whereunto ye do well that ye take heed, as
unto a light that shineth in a dark place, until
the day dawn, and the day star arise in your
hearts: Knowing this first, that no prophecy
of the scripture is of any private
interpretation. For the prophecy came not in
old time by the will of man: but holy men of
God spake as they were moved by the
Holy Ghost.

2 Peter 1:19—21

Ye are the body of Christ, and members in particular. And God hath set some in the church, first apostles, secondarily prophets, thirdly teachers, after that miracles, then gifts of healings, helps, governments, diversities of tongues.

1 Corinthians 12:27–28

Jesus said, "When he, the Spirit of truth, is come, he will guide you into all truth: for he shall not speak of himself; but whatsoever he shall hear, that shall he speak: and he will show you things to come."

John 16:13

Blessed is he that readeth, and they that hear the words of this prophecy, and keep those things which are written therein: for the time is at hand.

Revelation 1:3

PROTECTION

Thou shalt not be afraid for the terror by
night; nor for the arrow that flieth by day;
Nor for the pestilence that walketh in
darkness; nor for the destruction that
wasteth at noonday. A thousand shall fall at
thy side, and ten thousand at thy right hand;
but it shall not come nigh thee.

Psalm 91:5–7

Fear thou not; for I am with thee: be not
dismayed; for I am thy God: I will strengthen
thee; yea, I will help thee; yea, I will uphold
thee with the right hand of my righteousness.

Isaiah 41:10

The LORD is thy keeper: the LORD is thy
shade upon thy right hand. The sun shall not
smite thee by day, nor the moon by night.
The LORD shall preserve thee from all evil:
he shall preserve thy soul. The LORD shall
preserve thy going out and thy coming in
from this time forth, and even for evermore.

Psalm 121:5–8

Cast thy burden upon the LORD, and he shall sustain thee: he shall never suffer the righteous to be moved.

Psalm 55:22

The LORD preserveth all them that love him.

Psalm 145:20

I will say of the LORD, He is my refuge and my fortress: my God; in him will I trust. Surely he shall deliver thee from the snare of the fowler, and from the noisome pestilence. He shall cover thee with his feathers, and under his wings shalt thou trust: his truth shall be thy shield and buckler.

Psalm 91:2–4

God layeth up sound wisdom for the righteous: he is a buckler to them that walk uprightly. He keepeth the paths of judgment, and preserveth the way of his saints.

Proverbs 2:7–8

I will be glad and rejoice in thy mercy, Lord:
for thou hast considered my trouble; thou
hast known my soul in adversities; And hast
not shut me up into the hand of the enemy:
thou hast set my feet in a large room.

Psalm 31:7–8

The angel of the LORD encampeth round
about them that fear him, and delivereth them.

Psalm 34:7

The Lord shall deliver me from every evil
work, and will preserve me unto his heavenly
kingdom: to whom be glory for ever and ever.

2 Timothy 4:18

In thee, O LORD, do I put my trust: let me
never be put to confusion. Deliver me in thy
righteousness, and cause me to escape: incline
thine ear unto me, and save me. Be thou my
strong habitation, whereunto I may
continually resort: thou hast given
commandment to save me; for thou art my
rock and my fortress.

Psalm 71:1–3

The Lord is faithful, who shall stablish you,
and keep you from evil.

2 Thessalonians 3:3

Keep me as the apple of the eye, hide me
under the shadow of thy wings, O Lord.

Psalm 17:8

The eternal God is thy refuge, and
underneath are the everlasting arms.

Deuteronomy 33:27

In the fear of the LORD is strong confidence:
and his children shall have a place of refuge.

Proverbs 14:26

The LORD loveth judgment, and forsaketh
not his saints; they are preserved for ever.

Psalm 37:28

PROVISION

God hath given meat unto them that fear
him: he will ever be mindful of his covenant.

Psalm 111:5

God left not himself without witness, in that
he did good, and gave us rain from heaven,
and fruitful seasons, filling our hearts with
food and gladness.

Acts 14:17

God is able to make all grace abound toward
you; that ye, always having all sufficiency in
all things, may abound to every good work.

2 Corinthians 9:8

My God shall supply all your need according
to his riches in glory by Christ Jesus.

Philippians 4:19

My people shall be satisfied with my
goodness, saith the LORD.

Jeremiah 31:14

Jesus said, "Wherefore, if God so clothe the grass of the field, which to day is, and to morrow is cast into the oven, shall he not much more clothe you, O ye of little faith? Therefore take no thought, saying, What shall we eat? or, What shall we drink? or, Wherewithal shall we be clothed? ... for your heavenly Father knoweth that ye have need of all these things."

Matthew 6:30–32

Jesus said, "What man is there of you, whom if his son ask bread, will he give him a stone? Or if he ask a fish, will he give him a serpent? If ye then, being evil, know how to give good gifts unto your children, how much more shall your Father which is in heaven give good things to them that ask him?"

Matthew 7:9–11

The LORD shall guide thee continually, and satisfy thy soul in drought, and make fat thy bones: and thou shalt be like a watered garden, and like a spring of water, whose waters fail not.

Isaiah 58:11

God that ministereth seed to the sower both minister bread for your food, and multiply your seed sown, and increase the fruits of your righteousness; Being enriched in every thing to all bountifulness, which causeth through us thanksgiving to God.

2 Corinthians 9:10–11

I have been young, and now am old; yet have I not seen the righteous forsaken, nor his seed begging bread. He is ever merciful, and lendeth; and his seed is blessed.

Psalm 37:25–26

Jesus said, "Consider the ravens: for they neither sow nor reap; which neither have storehouse nor barn; and God feedeth them: how much more are ye better than the fowls?... Seek not ye what ye shall eat, or what ye shall drink, neither be ye of doubtful mind. For all these things do the nations of the world seek after: and your Father knoweth that ye have need of these things. But rather seek ye the kingdom of God; and all these things shall be added unto you."

Luke 12:24, 29–31

PURITY

He that loveth pureness of heart, for the grace of his lips the king shall be his friend.

Proverbs 22:11

Jesus said, "Blessed are the pure in heart: for they shall see God."

Matthew 5:8

Truly God is good to Israel, even to such as are of a clean heart.

Psalm 73:1

Whatsoever things are true, whatsoever things are honest, whatsoever things are just, whatsoever things are pure, whatsoever things are lovely, whatsoever things are of good report; if there be any virtue, and if there be any praise, think on these things.

Philippians 4:8

To be carnally minded is death; but to be
spiritually minded is life and peace.

Romans 8:6

The words of the LORD are pure words: as
silver tried in a furnace of earth, purified
seven times.

Psalm 12:6

The statutes of the LORD are right, rejoicing
the heart: the commandment of the LORD is
pure, enlightening the eyes.

Psalm 19:8

With the pure thou wilt show thyself pure,
O Lord.

Psalm 18:26

Pure religion and undefiled before God and
the Father is this, To visit the fatherless and
widows in their affliction, and to keep
himself unspotted from the world.

James 1:27

Who shall ascend into the hill of the LORD?
or who shall stand in his holy place? He that
hath clean hands, and a pure heart; who hath
not lifted up his soul unto vanity, nor sworn
deceitfully. He shall receive the blessing from
the LORD, and righteousness from the God
of his salvation.

Psalm 24:3–5

Thy word is very pure: therefore thy servant
loveth it, Lord.

Psalm 119:140

The words of the pure are pleasant words.

Proverbs 15:26

Every word of God is pure: he is a shield
unto them that put their trust in him.

Proverbs 30:5

PURPOSE

Jesus said, "This is the will of him that sent me, that every one which seeth the Son, and believeth on him, may have everlasting life: and I will raise him up at the last day."

John 6:40

So is the will of God, that with well doing ye may put to silence the ignorance of foolish men.

1 Peter 2:15

We are God's workmanship, created in Christ Jesus unto good works, which God hath before ordained that we should walk in them.

Ephesians 2:10

Be not conformed to this world: but be ye transformed by the renewing of your mind, that ye may prove what is that good, and acceptable, and perfect, will of God.

Romans 12:2

O come, let us worship and bow down: let us
kneel before the LORD our maker.
For he is our God; and we are the people of
his pasture, and the sheep of his hand.

Psalm 95:6—7

The LORD will not forsake his people for his
great name's sake: because it hath pleased
the LORD to make you his people.

1 Samuel 12:22

Put on therefore, as the elect of God, holy
and beloved, bowels of mercies, kindness,
humbleness of mind, meekness,
longsuffering;... Forbearing one another, and
forgiving one another,... even as Christ
forgave you, so also do ye.

Colossians 3:12—13

RECONCILIATION

Therefore if any man be in Christ, he is a new creature: old things are passed away; behold, all things are become new. All these things are of God, who hath reconciled us to himself by Jesus Christ, and hath given to us the ministry of reconciliation; To wit, that God was in Christ, reconciling the world unto himself, not imputing their trespasses unto them; and hath committed unto us the word of reconciliation.

2 Corinthians 5:17–19

Be ye kind one to another, tenderhearted, forgiving one another, even as God for Christ's sake hath forgiven you.

Ephesians 4:32

If ye forgive men their trespasses, your heavenly Father will also forgive you.

Matthew 6:14

Judge not, and ye shall not be judged:
condemn not, and ye shall not be
condemned: forgive, and ye shall be forgiven.

Luke 6:37

Jesus said, "When ye stand praying, forgive,
if ye have ought against any: that your Father
also which is in heaven may forgive you
your trespasses."

Mark 11:25

You, that were sometime alienated and
enemies in your mind by wicked works, yet
now hath Christ reconciled in the body of his
flesh through death, to present you holy and
unblameable and unreproveable in his sight.

Colossians 1:21–22

RELATIONSHIPS

Jesus said, "Behold, I stand at the door, and knock: if any man hear my voice, and open the door, I will come in to him, and will sup with him, and he with me."

Revelation 3:20

He that walketh with wise men shall be wise.

Proverbs 13:20

Jesus said, 'If ye abide in me, and my words abide in you, ye shall ask what ye will, and it shall be done unto you."

John 15:7

A man that hath friends must show himself friendly: and there is a friend that sticketh closer than a brother.

Proverbs 18:24

Jesus said, "Henceforth I call you not
servants for the servant knoweth not what
his lord doeth: but I have called you friends;
for all things that I have heard of my Father I
have made known unto you."

John 15:15

Faithful are the wounds of a friend; but the
kisses of an enemy are deceitful.

Proverbs 27:6

REPENTANCE

Repent, and be baptized every one of you in the name of Jesus Christ for the remission of sins, and ye shall receive the gift of the Holy Ghost.

Acts 2:38

Jesus said, "I say unto you, that likewise joy shall be in heaven over one sinner that repenteth, more than over ninety and nine just persons, which need no repentance."

Luke 15:7

Repent ye therefore, and be converted, that your sins may be blotted out, when the times of refreshing shall come from the presence of the Lord.

Acts 3:19

The Lord is not slack concerning his promise, as some men count slackness; but is longsuffering to us-ward, not willing that any should perish, but that all should come to repentance.

2 Peter 3:9

Thus saith the Lord GOD, the Holy One of
Israel; In returning and rest shall ye be saved;
in quietness and in confidence shall be
your strength.

Isaiah 30:15

Jesus said, "They that are whole need not a
physician; but they that are sick. I came
not to call the righteous, but sinners
to repentance."

Luke 5:31–32

Let the wicked forsake his way, and the
unrighteous man his thoughts: and let him
return unto the LORD, and he will have
mercy upon him; and to our God, for he will
abundantly pardon.

Isaiah 55:7

REST

The LORD is my shepherd; I shall not want. He maketh me to lie down in green pastures: he leadeth me beside the still waters. He restoreth my soul: he leadeth me in the paths of righteousness for his name's sake.

Psalm 23:1–3

Jesus said, "Come unto me, all ye that labour and are heavy laden, and I will give you rest. Take my yoke upon you, and learn of me; for I am meek and lowly in heart: and ye shall find rest unto your souls. For my yoke is easy, and my burden is light."

Matthew 11:28–30

God said, My presence shall go with thee, and I will give thee rest.

Exodus 33:14

"My people shall dwell in a peaceable habitation, and in sure dwellings, and in quiet resting places," saith the Lord.

Isaiah 32:18

Thus saith the LORD, Stand ye in the ways, and see, and ask for the old paths, where is the good way, and walk therein, and ye shall find rest for your souls.

Jeremiah 6:16

"I have satiated the weary soul, and I have replenished every sorrowful soul," saith the LORD.

Jeremiah 31:25

There remaineth ... a rest to the people of God. For he that is entered into his rest, he also hath ceased from his own works, as God did from his.

Hebrews 4:9–10

RESTORATION

O God, who is like unto thee! Thou, which hast showed me great and sore troubles, shalt quicken me again, and shalt bring me up again from the depths of the earth.

Psalm 71:19–20

The LORD upholdeth all that fall, and raiseth up all those that be bowed down.

Psalm 145:14

"I will restore to you the years that the locust hath eaten, the cankerworm, and the caterpillar, and the palmerworm, my great army which I sent among you. And ye shall eat in plenty, and be satisfied, and praise the name of the LORD your God, that hath dealt wondrously with you: and my people shall never be ashamed," saith the Lord.

Joel 2:25–26

Restore unto me the joy of thy salvation, O
Lord; and uphold me with thy free spirit.
Then will I teach transgressors thy ways; and
sinners shall be converted unto thee.

Psalm 51:12–13

I will seek that which was lost, and bring
again that which was driven away, and will
bind up that which was broken, and will
strengthen that which was sick, saith the
Lord GOD.

Ezekiel 34:16

If any man be in Christ, he is a new creature:
old things are passed away; behold, all things
are become new.

2 Corinthians 5:17

In Christ Jesus ye who sometimes were far
off are made nigh by the blood of Christ.

Ephesians 2:13

REVIVAL

The Spirit and the bride say, Come. And let him that heareth say, Come. And let him that is athirst come. And whosoever will, let him take the water of life freely.

Revelation 22:17

As many as received Jesus, to them gave he power to become the sons of God, even to them that believe on his name: Which were born, not of blood, nor of the will of the flesh, nor of the will of man, but of God.

John 1:12–13

I will give them one heart, and I will put a new spirit within you; and I will take the stony heart out of their flesh, and will give them an heart of flesh, saith the Lord.

Ezekiel 11:19

Wilt thou not revive us again: that thy people
may rejoice in thee? Show us thy mercy, O
LORD, and grant us thy salvation. ... Surely his
salvation is nigh them that fear him; that
glory may dwell in our land.

Psalm 85:6—7, 9

Though I walk in the midst of trouble, thou
wilt revive me, O Lord: thou shalt stretch
forth thine hand against the wrath of mine
enemies, and thy right hand shall save me.

Psalm 138:7

Thus saith the high and lofty One that
inhabiteth eternity, whose name is Holy; I
dwell in the high and holy place, with him
also that is of a contrite and humble spirit, to
revive the spirit of the humble, and to revive
the heart of the contrite ones.

Isaiah 57:15

REWARD

Jesus said, "Verily I say unto you, There is no man that hath left house, or brethren, or sisters, or father, or mother, or wife, or children, or lands, for my sake, and the gospel's, But he shall receive an hundredfold now in this time, houses, and brethren, and sisters, and mothers, and children, and lands, with persecutions; and in the world to come eternal life."

Mark 10:29–31

Jesus said, "Whosoever shall give to drink unto one of these little ones a cup of cold water only in the name of a disciple, verily I say unto you, he shall in no wise lose his reward."

Matthew 10:42

I the LORD search the heart, I try the reins, even to give every man according to his ways, and according to the fruit of his doings.

Jeremiah 17:10

According to the grace of God which is given unto me, as a wise masterbuilder, I have laid the foundation, and another buildeth theron. But let every man take heed how he buildeth thereupon. For other foundation can no man lay than that is laid, which is Jesus Christ. Now if any man build upon this foundation gold, silver, precious stones, wood, hay, stubble; Every man's work shall be made manifest: for the day shall declare it, because it shall be revealed by fire; and the fire shall try every man's work of what sort it is. If any man's work abide which he hath built thereupon, he shall receive a reward.

1 Corinthians 3:10–14

Jesus said, "Love ye your enemies, and do good, and lend, hoping for nothing again; and your reward shall be great, and ye shall be the children of the Highest."

Luke 6:35

Whatsoever good thing any man doeth, the same shall he receive of the Lord.

Ephesians 6:8

RIGHTEOUSNESS

Jesus said, "Blessed are they which are persecuted for righteousness' sake: for theirs is the kingdom of heaven."

Matthew 5:10

The LORD will not suffer the soul of the righteous to famish.

Proverbs 10:3

The fear of the wicked, it shall come upon him: but the desire of the righteous shall be granted. As the whirlwind passeth, so is the wicked no more: but the righteous is an everlasting foundation.

Proverbs 10:24—25

Thou, LORD, wilt bless the righteous; with favour wilt thou compass him as with a shield.

Psalm 5:12

Better is a little with righteousness than great revenues without right.

Proverbs 16:8

Blessed is the man that feareth the LORD,
that delighteth greatly in his commandments.
His seed shall be mighty upon earth: the
generation of the upright shall be blessed.
Wealth and riches shall be in his house: and
his righteousness endureth for ever.

Psalm 112:1—3

Treasures of wickedness profit nothing: but
righteousness delivereth from death.

Proverbs 10:2

A good man showeth favour, and lendeth:
he will guide his affairs with discretion.
Surely he shall not be moved for ever:
the righteous shall be in
everlasting remembrance.

Psalm 112:5—6

Jesus said, "Blessed are they which do hunger and thirst after righteousness: for they shall be filled."

Matthew 5:6

The work of righteousness shall be peace; and the effect of righteousness quietness and assurance for ever.

Isaiah 32:17

God hath made Christ to be sin for us, who knew no sin; that we might be made the righteousness of God in him.

2 Corinthians 5:21

He that followeth after righteousness and mercy findeth life, righteousness, and honour.

Proverbs 21:21

The LORD is righteous in all his ways, and holy in all his works.

Psalm 145:17

If any man sin, we have an advocate with the Father, Jesus Christ the righteous: And he is the propitiation for our sins: and not for ours only, but also for the sins of the whole world.

1 John 2:1–2

Now the righteousness of God without the law is manifested, being witnessed by the law and the prophets; even the righteousness of God which is by faith of Jesus Christ unto all and upon all them that believe.

Romans 3:21–22

As by one man's [Adam] disobedience many were made sinners, so by the obedience of one [Jesus] shall many be made righteous.

Romans 5:19

SACRIFICE

I beseech you therefore, brethren, by the mercies of God, that ye present your bodies a living sacrifice, holy, acceptable unto God, which is your reasonable service.

Romans 12:1

God so loved the world, that he gave his only begotten Son, that whosoever believeth in him should not perish, but have everlasting life.

John 3:16

By Christ therefore let us offer the sacrifice of praise to God continually, that is, the fruit of our lips giving thanks to his name. To do good and communicate forget not: for with such sacrifices God is well pleased.

Hebrews 13:15–16

Walk in love, as Christ also hath loved us, and hath given himself for us an offering and a sacrifice to God for a sweet-smelling savour.

Ephesians 5:2

Jesus, after he had offered one sacrifice for sins for ever, sat down on the right hand of God; From henceforth expecting till his enemies be made his footstool. For by one offering he hath perfected for ever them that are sanctified. Whereof the Holy Ghost also is a witness to us.

Hebrews 10:12–15

I will sacrifice unto thee, O God, with the voice of thanksgiving; I will pay that that I have vowed. Salvation is of the LORD.

Jonah 2:9

Let my prayer be set forth before thee, Lord, as incense; and the lifting up of my hands as the evening sacrifice.

Psalm 141:2

Oh that men would praise the LORD for his goodness, and for his wonderful works to the children of men! And let them sacrifice the sacrifices of thanksgiving, and declare his works with rejoicing.

Psalm 107:21–22

I will freely sacrifice unto thee: I will praise thy name, O LORD; for it is good. For he hath delivered me out of all trouble: and mine eye hath seen his desire upon mine enemies.

Psalm 54:6–7

The sacrifices of God are a broken spirit: a broken and a contrite heart, O God, thou wilt not despise.

Psalm 51:17

SALVATION

"Because he hath set his love upon me, therefore will I deliver him: I will set him on high, because he hath known my name. He shall call upon me, and I will answer him: I will be with him in trouble; I will deliver him, and honour him. With long life will I satisfy him, and show him my salvation," saith the Lord.

Psalm 91:14–16

There is one God, and one mediator between God and men, the man Christ Jesus; Who gave himself a ransom for all, to be testified in due time.

1 Timothy 2:5–6

God saith, I have heard thee in a time accepted, and in the day of salvation have I succoured thee: behold, now is the accepted time; behold, now is the day of salvation.

2 Corinthians 6:2

If thou shalt confess with thy mouth the Lord Jesus, and shalt believe in thine heart that God hath raised him from the dead, thou shalt be saved. For with the heart man believeth unto righteousness; and with the mouth confession is made unto salvation.

Romans 10:9–10

To Christ give all the prophets witness, that through his name whosoever believeth in him shall receive remission of sins.

Acts 10:43

Jesus said, "He that believeth and is baptized shall be saved."

Mark 16:16–18

Being made perfect, Christ became the author of eternal salvation unto all them that obey him.

Hebrews 5:9

Behold, the eye of the LORD is upon them
that fear him, upon them that hope in his
mercy; To deliver their soul from death, and
to keep them alive in famine.

Psalm 33:18—19

The angel of the LORD encampeth round
about them that fear him, and delivereth them.

Psalm 34:7

God sent not his Son into the world to
condemn the world; but that the world
through him might be saved.

John 3:17

Jesus said, "I am the door: by me if any man
enter in, he shall be saved, and shall go in and
out, and find pasture."

John 10:9

Look unto me, and be ye saved, all the ends of the earth: for I am God, and there is none else.

Isaiah 45:22

Salvation belongeth unto the LORD: thy blessing is upon thy people.

Psalm 3:8

Fear ye not, stand still, and see the salvation of the LORD, which he will show to you today.

Exodus 14:13

The LORD is my strength and song, and he is become my salvation: he is my God, and I will prepare him an habitation; my father's God, and I will exalt him.

Exodus 15:2

SECURITY

We may boldly say, The Lord is my helper, and I will not fear what man shall do unto me.

Hebrews 13:6

The LORD is the portion of mine inheritance and of my cup: thou maintainest my lot.

Psalm 16:5

Who is he that will harm you, if ye be followers of that which is good?

1 Peter 3:13

I am persuaded, that neither death, nor life, nor angels, nor principalities, nor powers, nor things present, nor things to come, Nor height, nor depth, nor any other creature, shall be able to separate us from the love of God, which is in Christ Jesus our Lord.

Romans 8:38—39

They that know thy name will put their trust in thee: for thou, LORD, hast not forsaken them that seek thee.

Psalm 9:10

They that trust in the Lord shall be as mount Zion, which cannot be removed, but abideth forever.

Psalm 125:1

The name of the LORD is a strong tower: the righteous runneth into it, and is safe.

Proverbs 18:10

"Wherefore ye shall do my statutes, and keep my judgments, and do them; and ye shall dwell in the land in safety. And the land shall yield her fruit, and ye shall eat your fill, and dwell therein in safety," saith the Lord.

Leviticus 25:18–19

SELF-CONTROL

Jesus said unto his disciples, If any man will come after me, let him deny himself, and take up his cross, and follow me.

Matthew 16:24

There hath no temptation taken you but such as is common to man: but God is faithful, who will not suffer you to be tempted above that ye are able; but will with the temptation also make a way to escape, that ye may be able to bear it.

1 Corinthians 10:13

My beloved brethren, be ye stedfast, unmoveable, always abounding in the work of the Lord, forasmuch as ye know that your labour is not in vain in the Lord.

1 Corinthians 15:58

Jesus said, "Behold, I come quickly: hold that fast which thou hast, that no man take thy crown."

Revelation 3:11

Take heed to thyself, and keep thy soul
diligently, lest thou forget the things which
thine eyes have seen, and lest they depart
from thy heart all the days of thy life: but
teach them thy sons, and thy sons' sons.

Deuteronomy 4:9

Not by works of righteousness which we have
done, but according to his mercy he saved us,
by the washing of regeneration, and renewing
of the Holy Ghost; Which he shed on us
abundantly through Jesus Christ our Saviour;
That being justified by his grace, we should
be made heirs according to the hope of
eternal life. This is a faithful saying, and
these things I will that thou affirm
constantly, that they which have believed in
God might be careful to maintain good
works. These things are good and profitable
unto men.

Titus 3:5—8

SELF-ESTEEM

"Can a woman forget her sucking child, that she should not have compassion on the son of her womb? yea, they may forget, yet will I not forget thee. Behold, I have graven thee upon the palms of my hands; thy walls are continually before me," saith the Lord.

Isaiah 49:15—16

Jesus said, "Are not two sparrows sold for a farthing? and one of them shall not fall on the ground without your Father. But the very hairs of your head are all numbered. Fear ye not therefore, ye are of more value than many sparrows."

Matthew 10:29—31

God hath chosen us in Christ before the foundation of the world, that we should be holy and without blame before him in love: Having predestinated us unto the adoption of children by Jesus Christ to himself.

Ephesians 1:4—5

Know ye that the LORD he is God: it is he that
hath made us, and not we ourselves;
we are his people, and the sheep of his pasture.

Psalm 100:3

The LORD hath appeared of old unto me,
saying, Yea, I have loved thee with an
everlasting love: therefore with
lovingkindness have I drawn thee.

Jeremiah 31:3

Having therefore, brethren, boldness to enter
into the holiest by the blood of Jesus, ... let us
draw near with a true heart in full assurance
of faith, having our hearts sprinkled from an
evil conscience, and our bodies washed with
pure water.

Hebrews 10:19, 22

SPEECH

The words of wise men are heard in quiet
more than the cry of him that ruleth
among fools.

Ecclesiastes 9:17

A wholesome tongue is a tree of life.

Proverbs 15:4

If any man speak, let him speak as the oracles
of God; if any man minister, let him do it as
of the ability which God giveth: that God in
all things may be glorified through Jesus
Christ, to whom be praise and dominion for
ever and ever.

1 Peter 4:11

Whoso keepeth his mouth and his tongue
keepeth his soul from troubles.

Proverbs 21:23

Speaking the truth in love, ... grow up into
him in all things, which is the head,
even Christ.

Ephesians 4:15

Pleasant words are as an honeycomb, sweet
to the soul, and health to the bones.

Proverbs 16:24

He that speaketh truth showeth
forth righteousness.

Proverbs 12:17

Righteous lips are the delight of kings; and
they love him that speaketh right.

Proverbs 16:13

STEWARDSHIP

As every man hath received the gift, even so minister the same one to another, as good stewards of the manifold grace of God.

1 Peter 4:10

[Jesus told this parable]: A certain nobleman went into a far country to receive for himself a kingdom, and to return. And he called his ten servants, and delivered them ten pounds, and said unto them, Occupy till I come. ... And it came to pass, that when he was returned, having received the kingdom, then he commanded these servants to be called unto him, to whom he had given the money, that he might know how much every man had gained by trading. Then came the first, saying, Lord, thy pound hath gained ten pounds. And he said unto him, Well, thou good servant: because thou hast been faithful in a very little, have thou authority over ten cities. And the second came, saying, Lord, thy pound hath gained five pounds. And he said likewise to him, Be thou also over five cities. ... For I say unto you, That unto every one which hath shall be given.

Luke 19:12–13, 15–19, 26

STRENGTH

God giveth power to the faint; and to them
that have no might he increaseth strength.
Even the youths shall faint and be weary, and
the young men shall utterly fall: But they that
wait upon the LORD shall renew their
strength; they shall mount up with wings as
eagles; they shall run, and not be weary; and
they shall walk, and not faint.

Isaiah 40:29–31

Fear thou not; for I am with thee: be not
dismayed; for I am thy God: I will strengthen
thee; yea, I will help thee; yea, I will uphold
thee with the right hand of my righteousness.

Isaiah 41:10

Blessed is the man whose strength is in thee,
O Lord; in whose heart are the ways of them.

Psalm 84:5

God is our refuge and strength, a very
present help in trouble.

Psalm 46:1

I will love thee, O LORD, my strength. The
LORD is my rock, and my fortress, and my
deliverer; my God, my strength, in whom I
will trust; my buckler, and the horn of my
salvation, and my high tower.

Psalm 18:1–2

Know I that the LORD saveth his anointed;
he will hear him from his holy heaven with
the saving strength of his right hand.

Psalm 20:6

The salvation of the righteous is of the
LORD: he is their strength in the time
of trouble.

Psalm 37:39

STRUGGLE

I would that ye knew what great conflict I have for you, and for them at Laodicea, and for as many as have not seen my face in the flesh; That their hearts might be comforted, being knit together in love, and unto all riches of the full assurance of understanding, to the acknowledgement of the mystery of God, and of the Father, and of Christ; In whom are hid all the treasures of wisdom and knowledge.

Colossians 2:1–3

What shall I more say? for the time would fail me to tell of Gedeon, and of Barak, and of Samson, and of Jephthae; of David also, and Samuel, and of the prophets: Who through faith subdued kingdoms, wrought righteousness, obtained promises, stopped the mouths of lions, Quenched the violence of fire, escaped the edge of the sword, out of weakness were made strong, waxed valiant in fight, turned to flight the armies of the aliens. ... of whom the world was not worthy.

Hebrews 11:32–34, 38

Being justified by faith, we have peace with God through our Lord Jesus Christ: By whom also we have access by faith into this grace wherein we stand, and rejoice in hope of the glory of God. And not only so, but we glory in tribulations also: knowing that tribulation worketh patience; And patience, experience; and experience, hope: And hope maketh not ashamed; because the love of God is shed abroad in our hearts by the Holy Ghost which is given unto us.

Romans 5:1—5

A great multitude, which no man could number, of all nations, and kindreds, and people, and tongues, stood before the throne, and before the Lamb, clothed with white robes, and palms in their hands. ... These are they which came out of great tribulation, and have washed their robes, and made them white in the blood of the Lamb. Therefore are they before the throne of God, and serve him day and night in his temple: and he that sitteth on the throne shall dwell among them.

Revelation 7:9, 14—15

With God all things are possible.

Matthew 19:26

We ourselves glory in you in the churches of
God for your patience and faith in all your
persecutions and tribulations that ye endure:
Which is a manifest token of the righteous
judgment of God, that ye may be counted
worthy of the kingdom of God, for which ye
also suffer.

2 Thessalonians 1:4–5

When thou art in tribulation, and all these
things are come upon thee, ... if thou turn to
the LORD thy God, and shalt be obedient
unto his voice; (For the LORD thy God is a
merciful God;) he will not forsake thee,
neither destroy thee, nor forget the covenant
of thy fathers which he sware unto them.

Deuteronomy 4:30–31

SUCCESS

Humility and the fear of the LORD are riches, and honour, and life.

Proverbs 22:4

[Wisdom spoke]: "Riches and honour are with me; yea, durable riches and righteousness. My fruit is better than gold, yea, than fine gold; and my revenue than choice silver. I lead in the way of righteousness, in the midst of the paths of judgment: That I may cause those that love me to inherit substance; and I will fill their treasures."

Proverbs 8:18—21

The LORD . . . grant thee according to thine own heart, and fulfil all thy counsel.

Psalm 20:4

Without counsel purposes are disappointed: but in the multitude of counsellors they are established.

Proverbs 15:22

Blessed is the man that walketh not in the counsel of the ungodly, nor standeth in the way of sinners, nor sitteth in the seat of the scornful. But his delight is in the law of the LORD; and in his law doth he meditate day and night. And he shall be like a tree planted by the rivers of water, that bringeth forth his fruit in his season; his leaf also shall not wither; and whatsoever he doeth shall prosper.

Psalm 1:1–3

Commit thy works unto the LORD, and thy thoughts shall be established.

Proverbs 16:3

Promotion cometh neither from the east, nor from the west, nor from the south. But God is the judge: he putteth down one, and setteth up another.

Psalm 75:6–7

Let them shout for joy, and be glad, that
favour my righteous cause: yea, let them say
continually, Let the LORD be magnified,
which hath pleasure in the prosperity of
his servant.

Psalm 35:27

Believe in the LORD your God, so shall ye be
established; believe his prophets, so shall
ye prosper.

2 Chronicles 20:20

This book of the law shall not depart out of
thy mouth; but thou shalt meditate therein
day and night, that thou mayest observe to
do according to all that is written therein: for
then thou shalt make thy way prosperous,
and then thou shalt have good success.

Joshua 1:8

He becometh poor that dealeth with a
slack hand: but the hand of the diligent
maketh rich.

Proverbs 10:4

He that covereth his sins shall not prosper:
but whoso confesseth and forsaketh them
shall have mercy.

Proverbs 28:13

It shall come to pass, if thou shalt hearken
diligently unto the voice of the LORD thy
God, to observe and to do all his
commandments which I command thee this
day, that the LORD thy God will set thee on
high above all nations of the earth: And all
these blessings shall come on thee, and
overtake thee, if thou shalt hearken unto the
voice of the LORD thy God.... The LORD
shall command the blessing upon thee in thy
storehouses, and in all that thou settest thine
hand unto; and he shall bless thee in the land
which the LORD thy God giveth thee.

Deuteronomy 28:1–2, 8

SUFFERING

The righteous cry, and the LORD heareth,
and delivereth them out of all their troubles.

Psalm 34:17

God is our refuge and strength, a very
present help in trouble.

Psalm 46:1

Many are the afflictions of the righteous: but
the LORD delivereth him out of them all.

Psalm 34:19

Weeping may endure for a night, but joy
cometh in the morning.

Psalm 30:5

I sought the LORD, and he heard me, and
delivered me from all my fears.

Psalm 34:4

God healeth the broken in heart, and
bindeth up their wounds.

Psalm 147:3

"As one whom his mother comforteth, so will
I comfort you," saith the Lord.

Isaiah 66:13

Who shall separate us from the love of
Christ? shall tribulation, or distress, or
persecution, or famine, or nakedness, or peril,
or sword? ... Nay, in all these things we are
more than conquerors through him that
loved us.

Romans 8:35, 37

God hath not despised nor abhorred the
affliction of the afflicted; neither hath he hid
his face from him; but when he cried unto
him, he heard.

Psalm 22:24

When thou art in tribulation, ... if thou turn
to the LORD thy God, and shalt be obedient
unto his voice; (For the LORD thy God is a
merciful God;) he will not forsake thee,
neither destroy thee, nor forget the covenant
of thy fathers which he sware unto them.

Deuteronomy 4:30–31

As the sufferings of Christ abound in us, so
our consolation also aboundeth by Christ.
And whether we be afflicted, it is for your
consolation and salvation, which is effectual
in the enduring of the same sufferings which
we also suffer: or whether we be comforted,
it is for your consolation and salvation.

2 Corinthians 1:5–6

Whether we live, we live unto the Lord; and
whether we die, we die unto the Lord:
whether we live therefore, or die, we are
the Lord's.

Romans 14:8

God shall wipe away all tears from [the
believers'] eyes; and there shall be no more
death, neither sorrow, nor crying, neither
shall there be any more pain: for the former
things are passed away.

Revelation 21:4

TALENTS AND GIFTS

Every good gift and every perfect gift is from above, and cometh down from the Father of lights, with whom is no variableness, neither shadow of turning.

James 1:17

A man's gift maketh room for him, and bringeth him before great men.

Proverbs 18:16

As every man hath received the gift, even so minister the same one to another; as good stewards of the manifold grace of God. If any man speak, let him speak as the oracles of God; if any man minister, let him do it as of the ability which God giveth; that God in all things may be glorified through Jesus Christ, to whom be praise and dominion for ever and ever.

1 Peter 4:10—11

There are diversities of gifts, but the same
Spirit. And there are differences of
administrations, but the same Lord. And
there are diversities of operations, but it is
the same God which worketh all in all. But
the manifestation of the Spirit is given to
every man to profit withal.

1 Corinthians 12:4—7

A gift is as a precious stone in the eyes of
him that hath it: whithersoever it turneth,
it prospereth.

Proverbs 17:8

The wages of sin is death; but the gift of God
is eternal life through Jesus Christ our Lord.

Romans 6:23

TEMPTATION

There hath no temptation taken you but
such as is common to man: but God is
faithful, who will not suffer you to be
tempted above that ye are able; but will with
the temptation also make a way to escape,
that ye may be able to bear it.

1 Corinthians 10:13

In that Jesus himself hath suffered being
tempted, he is able to succour them that
are tempted.

Hebrews 2:18

Take unto you the whole armour of God, that
ye may be able to withstand in the evil day,
and having done all, to stand.

Ephesians 6:13

Jesus said, "Because thou hast kept the word
of my patience, I also will keep thee from the
hour of temptation, which shall come upon
all the world, to try them that dwell upon
the earth."

Revelation 3:10

We have not an high priest which cannot be touched with the feeling of our infirmities, but was in all points tempted like as we are, yet without sin. Let us therefore come boldly unto the throne of grace, that we may obtain mercy, and find grace to help in time of need.

Hebrews 4:15–16

Brethren, if a man be overtaken in a fault, ye which are spiritual, restore such an one in the spirit of meekness; considering thyself, lest thou also be tempted. Bear ye one another's burdens, and so fulfil the law of Christ.

Galatians 6:1–2

Blessed is the man that endureth temptation: for when he is tried, he shall receive the crown of life, which the Lord hath promised to them that love him.

James 1:12

THANKFULNESS

O give thanks unto the LORD, for he is good:
for his mercy endureth for ever.

Psalm 107:1

In every thing give thanks: for this is the will
of God in Christ Jesus concerning you.

1 Thessalonians 5:18

The LORD is my strength and my shield; my
heart trusted in him, and I am helped:
therefore my heart greatly rejoiceth; and with
my song will I praise him.

Psalm 28:7

Enter into God's gates with thanksgiving, and
into his courts with praise: be thankful unto
him, and bless his name. For the LORD is
good; his mercy is everlasting; and his truth
endureth to all generations.

Psalm 100:4—5

Thanks be to God, which giveth us the
victory through our Lord Jesus Christ.

1 Corinthians 15:57

I exhort ... that, first of all, supplications,
prayers, intercessions, and giving of thanks,
be made for all men; for kings, and for all
that are in authority; that we may lead a quiet
and peaceable life in all godliness and
honesty. For this is good and acceptable in
the sight of God our Saviour.

1 Timothy 2:1–3

For every creature of God is good, and
nothing to be refused, if it be received with
thanksgiving: For it is sanctified by the word
of God and prayer.

1 Timothy 4:4–5

Let us come before God's presence with
thanksgiving, and make a joyful noise unto
him with psalms. ... For he is our God; and we
are the people of his pasture, and the sheep
of his hand.

Psalm 95:2, 7

I will praise the name of God with a song,
and will magnify him with thanksgiving. This
also shall please the LORD better than an ox
or bullock that hath horns and hoofs. The
humble shall see this, and be glad: and your
heart shall live that seek God.

Psalm 69:30–32

O give thanks unto the Lord; for he is good;
for his mercy endureth for ever. O give
thanks unto the God of gods, for his mercy
endureth for ever. O give thanks to the Lord
of lords: for his mercy endureth for ever.

Psalm 136:1–3

Let us offer the sacrifice of praise to God
continually, that is, the fruit of our lips giving
thanks to his name.

Hebrews 13:15

We are bound to give thanks always to God
for you, brethren beloved of the Lord,
because God hath from the beginning chosen
you to salvation through sanctification of the
Spirit and belief of the truth; Whereunto he
called you by our gospel, to the obtaining of
the glory of our Lord Jesus Christ.

2 Thessalonians 2:13–14

Thanks be unto God, which always causeth
us to triumph in Christ, and makest manifest
the savour of his knowledge by us in
every place.

2 Corinthians 2:14

TIME

Of old hast thou laid the foundation of the earth, O God: and the heavens are the work of thy hands.

Psalm 102:25

Jesus said unto [his disciples], "It is not for you to know the times or the seasons, which the Father hath put in his own power. But ye shall receive power, after that the Holy Ghost is come upon you: and ye shall be witnesses unto me both in Jerusalem, and in all Judaea,. and in Samaria, and unto the uttermost part of the earth."

Acts 1:7–8

Jesus said, "Behold, I come quickly: hold that fast which thou hast, that no man take thy crown."

Revelation 3:11

To every thing there is a season, and a time
to every purpose under the heaven:
A time to be born, and a time to die; a time
to plant, and a time to pluck up that which
is planted;
A time to kill, and a time to heal; a time to
break down, and a time to build up;
A time to weep, and a time to laugh; a time
to mourn, and a time to dance;
A time to cast away stones, and a time to
gather stones together; a time to embrace,
and a time to refrain from embracing;
A time to get, and a time to lose; a time to
keep, and a time to cast away;
A time to rend, and a time to sew; a time to
keep silence, and a time to speak;
A time to love, and a time to hate; a time of
war, and a time of peace.

Ecclesiastes 3:1–8

TITHES AND OFFERINGS

Bring ye all the tithes into the storehouse, that there may be meat in mine house, and prove me now herewith, saith the LORD of hosts, if I will not open you the windows of heaven, and pour you out a blessing, that there shall not be room enough to receive it.

Malachi 3:10

Honour the LORD with thy substance, and with the firstfruits of all thine increase: So shall thy barns be filled with plenty, and thy presses shall burst out with new wine.

Proverbs 3:9–10

Jesus said, "Give, and it shall be given unto you; good measure, pressed down, and shaken together, and running over, shall men give into your bosom. For with the same measure that ye mete withal it shall be measured to you again."

Luke 6:38

All the tithe of the land, whether of the seed
of the land, or of the fruit of the tree, is the
LORD'S: it is holy unto the LORD.

Leviticus 27:30

The LORD preserveth the simple: I was
brought low, and he helped me. ... What shall
I render unto the LORD for all his benefits
toward me? ... I will offer to thee the sacrifice
of thanksgiving, and will call upon the name
of the LORD.

Psalm 116:6, 12, 17

Whatsoever a man soweth, that shall he
also reap.

Galatians 6:7

TROUBLE

The righteous cry, and the LORD heareth,
and delivereth them out of all their troubles.

Psalm 34:17

The Spirit also helpeth our infirmities: for
we know not what we should pray for as we
ought: but the Spirit itself maketh
intercession for us with groanings which
cannot be uttered. And he that searcheth the
hearts knoweth what is the mind of the
Spirit, because he maketh intercession for the
saints according to the will of God.

Romans 8:26—27

Blessed be God, even the Father of our Lord
Jesus Christ, the Father of mercies, and the
God of all comfort; Who comforteth us in all
our tribulation, that we may be able to
comfort them which are in any trouble, by
the comfort wherewith we ourselves are
comforted of God. For as the sufferings of
Christ abound in us, so our consolation also
aboundeth by Christ.

2 Corinthians 1:3—5

I reckon that the sufferings of this present
time are not worthy to be compared with the
glory which shall be revealed in us.

Romans 8:18

If ye be reproached for the name of Christ,
happy are ye; for the spirit of glory and of
God resteth upon you.

1 Peter 4:14

My brethren, count it all joy when ye fall into
divers temptations; Knowing this, that the
trying of your faith worketh patience. But let
patience have her perfect work, that ye may
be perfect and entire, wanting nothing.

James 1:2–4

Many are the afflictions of the righteous: but
the LORD delivereth him out of them all.

Psalm 34:19

I take pleasure in infirmities, in reproaches,
in necessities, in persecutions, in distresses
for Christ's sake: for when I am weak, then
am I strong.

2 Corinthians 12:10

Blessed is the man that endureth temptation:
for when he is tried, he shall receive the
crown of life, which the Lord hath promised
to them that love him.

James 1:12

We wrestle not against flesh and blood, but
against principalities, against powers, against
the rulers of the darkness in this world,
against spiritual wickedness in high places.
Wherefore take unto you the whole armour
of God, that ye may be able to withstand in
the evil day, and having done all, to stand.

Ephesians 6:12–13

Thou hast been a strength to the poor, a strength to the needy in his distress, a refuge from the storm, a shadow from the heat, O Lord.

Isaiah 25:4

Because thou hast made the LORD, which is my refuge, even the most High, thy habitation; There shall no evil befall thee, neither shall any plague come nigh thy dwelling. For he shall give his angels charge over thee, to keep thee in all thy ways. They shall bear thee up in their hands, lest thou dash thy foot against a stone.

Psalm 91:9–12

"He shall call upon me, and I will answer him: I will be with him in trouble; I will deliver him, and honour him. With long life will I satisfy him, and show him my salvation," saith the Lord.

Psalm 91:15–16

God is our refuge and strength, a very
present help in trouble. Therefore will not
we fear, though the earth be removed, and
though the mountains be carried into the
midst of the sea; though the waters thereof
roar and be troubled, though the mountains
shake with the swelling thereof.

Psalm 46:1–3

The wicked is snared by the transgression
of his lips; but the just shall come out
of trouble.

Proverbs 12:13

Though I walk in the midst of trouble, thou
wilt revive me: thou shalt stretch forth thine
hand against the wrath of mine enemies, and
thy right hand shall save me, O Lord.

Psalm 138:7

TRUST

Thou wilt keep him in perfect peace, whose mind is stayed on thee: because he trusteth in thee. Trust ye in the LORD for ever: for in the LORD JEHOVAH is everlasting strength.

Isaiah 26:3–4

He that trusteth in his own heart is a fool: but whoso walketh wisely, he shall be delivered.

Proverbs 28:26

They that know thy name will put their trust in thee: for thou, LORD, hast not forsaken them that seek thee.

Psalm 9:10

He that is of a proud heart stirreth up strife: but he that putteth his trust in the LORD shall be made fat.

Proverbs 28:25

Blessed is the man that trusteth in the LORD,
and whose hope the LORD is.

Jeremiah 17:7

As for God, his way is perfect: the word of
the LORD is tried: he is a buckler to all those
that trust in him.

Psalm 18:30

The fear of man bringeth a snare: but whoso
putteth his trust in the LORD shall be safe.

Proverbs 29:25

Trust in the LORD, and do good; so shalt
thou dwell in the land, and verily thou shalt
be fed.

Psalm 37:3

They that trust in the LORD shall be as
mount Zion, which cannot be removed, but
abideth for ever.

Psalm 125:1

We should be to the praise of God's glory,
who first trusted in Christ. In whom ye also
trusted, after that ye heard the word of truth,
the gospel of your salvation: in whom also
after that ye believed, ye were sealed with
that holy Spirit of promise, Which is the
earnest of our inheritance until the
redemption of the purchased possession,
unto the praise of his glory.

Ephesians 1:12—14

Be merciful unto me, O God, be merciful
unto me: for my soul trusteth in thee: yea, in
the shadow of thy wings will I make my
refuge, until these calamities be overpast. I
will cry unto God most high; unto God that
performeth all things for me.

Psalm 57:1—2

He that handleth a matter wisely shall find
good: and whoso trusteth in the LORD, happy
is he.

Proverbs 16:20

Judge me, O LORD; for I have walked in mine integrity: I have trusted also in the LORD; therefore I shall not slide.

Psalm 26:1

Many sorrows shall be to the wicked: but he that trusteth in the LORD, mercy shall compass him about.

Psalm 32:10

O taste and see that the LORD is good: blessed is the man that trusteth in him. O fear the LORD, ye his saints: for there is no want to them that fear him.

Psalm 34:8–9

Every word of God is pure: he is a shield unto them that put their trust in him.

Proverbs 30:5

The LORD is my strength and my shield; my heart trusted in him, and I am helped: therefore my heart greatly rejoiceth; and with my song will I praise him.

Psalm 28:7

"He that putteth his trust in me shall possess the land, and shall inherit my holy mountain," saith the Lord.

Isaiah 57:13

The salvation of the righteous is of the LORD: he is their strength in the time of trouble. The LORD shall help them, and deliver them: he shall deliver them from the wicked, and save them, because they trust in him.

Psalm 37:40

TRUTH

Jesus said, "Thou sayest that I am a king. To this end was I born, and for this cause came I into the world, that I should bear witness unto the truth. Every one that is of the truth heareth my voice."

John 18:37

LORD, who shall abide in thy tabernacle? who shall dwell in thy holy hill? He that walketh uprightly, and worketh righteousness, and speaketh the truth in his heart.

Psalm 15:1–2

He that speaketh truth showeth forth righteousness.

Proverbs 12:17

The LORD is nigh unto all them that call upon him, to all that call upon him in truth.

Psalm 145:18

Jesus said, "I am the way, the truth, and the
life: no man cometh unto the Father,
but by me."

John 14:6

We know that the Son of God is come, and
hath given us an understanding, that we may
know him that is true, and we are in him that
is true, even in his Son Jesus Christ. This is
the true God, and eternal life.

1 John 5:20

Ye shall know the truth, and the truth shall
make you free.

John 8:32

Thy word is true from the beginning,
O Lord: and every one of thy righteous
judgments endureth for ever.

Psalm 119:160

He that walketh righteously, and speaketh
uprightly; he that despiseth the gain of
oppressions, that shaketh his hands from
holding of bribes, that stoppeth his ears from
hearing of blood, and shutteth his eyes from
seeing evil; He shall dwell on high: his place
of defence shall be the munitions of rocks:
bread shall be given him; his waters shall
be sure.

Isaiah 33:15—16

The word of the LORD is right; and all his
works are done in truth. He loveth
righteousness and judgment: the earth is full
of the goodness of the LORD.

Psalm 33:4—5

Thou, O Lord, art a God full of compassion,
and gracious, longsuffering, and plenteous in
mercy and truth.

Psalm 86:15

The fear of the LORD is clean, enduring for ever: the judgments of the LORD are true and righteous altogether. More to be desired are they than gold, yea, than much fine gold: sweeter also than honey and the honeycomb.

Psalm 19:9—10

A true witness delivereth souls.

Proverbs 14:25

The LORD is the true God, he is the living God, and an everlasting king.

Jeremiah 10:10

UNITY

Ye are a chosen generation, a royal
priesthood, an holy nation, a peculiar people;
that ye should show forth the praises of him
who hath called you out of darkness into his
marvellous light: Which in time past were
not a people, but are now the people of God:
which had not obtained mercy, but now have
obtained mercy.

1 Peter 2:9—10

Keep the unity of the Spirit in the bond of
peace. There is one body, and one Spirit,
even as ye are called in one hope of your
calling; one Lord, one faith, one baptism,
One God and Father of all, who is above all,
and through all, and in you all.

Ephesians 4:3—6

Behold, how good and how pleasant it is for
brethren to dwell together in unity!

Psalm 133:1

He that loveth his brother abideth in the light, and there is none occasion of stumbling in him.

1 John 2:10

Beloved, let us love one another: for love is of God; and every one that loveth is born of God, and knoweth God.

1 John 4:7

God gave some, apostles; and some, prophets; and some, evangelists; and some, pastors and teachers; For the perfecting of the saints, for the work of the ministry, for the edifying of the body of Christ: Till we all come in the unity of the faith, and of the knowledge of the Son of God, unto a perfect man, unto the measure of the stature of the fulness of Christ.

Ephesians 4:11—13

VICTORY

Whatsoever is born of God overcometh the world: and this is the victory that overcometh the world, even our faith. Who is he that overcometh the world, but he that believeth that Jesus is the Son of God?

1 John 5:4–5

In a moment, in the twinkling of an eye, at the last trump: for the trumpet shall sound, and the dead shall be raised incorruptible, and we shall be changed. ... So when this corruptible shall have put on incorruption, and this mortal shall have put on immortality, then shall be brought to pass the saying that is written, Death is swallowed up in victory. O death, where is thy sting? O grave, where is thy victory? The sting of death is sin; and the strength of sin is the law. But thanks be to God, which giveth the victory through our Lord Jesus Christ.

1 Corinthians 15:52, 54–57

The LORD will swallow up death in victory; and the Lord GOD will wipe away tears from off all faces; and the rebuke of his people shall he take away from off all the earth: for the LORD hath spoken it. And it shall be said in that day, Lo, this is our God; we have waited for him, and he will save us: this is the LORD; we have waited for him, we will be glad and rejoice in his salvation.

Isaiah 25:8—9

O sing unto the LORD a new song; for he hath done marvellous things: his right hand, and his holy arm, hath gotten him the victory.

Psalm 98:1

A bruised reed shall God not break, and smoking flax shall he not quench, till he send forth judgment unto victory.

Matthew 12:20

WISDOM

If any of you lack wisdom, let him ask of
God, that giveth to all men liberally, and
upbraideth not; and it shall be given him.

James 1:5

God giveth to a man that is good in his sight
wisdom, and knowledge, and joy.

Ecclesiastes 2:26

Happy is the man that findeth wisdom, and
the man that getteth understanding. For the
merchandise of it is better than the
merchandise of silver, and the gain thereof
than fine gold.

Proverbs 3:13–14

Wisdom is the principal thing; therefore get
wisdom: and with all thy getting get
understanding. Exalt her, and she shall
promote thee: she shall bring thee to honour,
when thou dost embrace her.

Proverbs 4:7–8

So shall the knowledge of wisdom be unto thy soul: when thou hast found it, then there shall be a reward, and thy expectation shall not be cut off.

Proverbs 24:14

Wisdom is good with an inheritance: and by it there is profit to them that see the sun. For wisdom is a defence, and money is a defence: but the excellency of knowledge is, that wisdom giveth life to them that have it.

Ecclesiastes 7:11–12

Behold, God desireth truth in the inward parts: and in the hidden part God shall make me to know wisdom.

Psalm 51:6

The wisdom that is from above is first pure, then peaceable, gentle, and easy to be entreated, full of mercy and good fruits, without partiality, and without hypocrisy.

James 3:17

Who is as the wise man? and who knoweth the interpretation of a thing? a man's wisdom maketh his face to shine, and the boldness of his face shall be changed.

Ecclesiastes 8:1

The fear of the LORD is the beginning of wisdom: a good understanding have all they that do his commandments: his praise endureth for ever.

Psalm 111:10

The LORD giveth wisdom: out of his mouth cometh knowledge and understanding. He layeth up sound wisdom for the righteous.

Proverbs 2:6—7

He that getteth wisdom loveth his own soul: he that keepeth understanding shall find good.

Proverbs 19:8

When wisdom entereth into thine heart, and knowledge is pleasant unto thy soul;
Discretion shall preserve thee, understanding shall keep thee.

Proverbs 2:10

Teach us to number our days, that we may apply our hearts unto wisdom, O Lord.

Psalm 90:12

When pride cometh, then cometh shame: but with the lowly is wisdom.

Proverbs 11:2

Wisdom strengtheneth the wise more than ten mighty men which are in the city.

Ecclesiastes 7:19

WORK

Whatsoever ye do, do it heartily, as to the Lord, and not unto men; Knowing that of the Lord ye shall receive the reward of the inheritance: for ye serve the Lord Christ.

Colossians 3:23—24

Wealth gotten by vanity shall be diminished: but he that gathereth by labour shall increase.

Proverbs 13:11

It is good and comely for one to eat and to drink, and to enjoy the good of all his labour that he taketh under the sun all the days of his life, which God giveth him: for it is his portion. Every man also to whom God hath given riches and wealth, and hath given him power to eat thereof, and to take his portion, and to rejoice in his labour; this is the gift of God.

Ecclesiastes 5:18—19

He becometh poor that dealeth with a
slack hand: but the hand of the diligent
maketh rich.

Proverbs 10:4

My beloved brethren, be ye stedfast,
unmoveable, always abounding in the work of
the Lord, forasmuch as ye know that your
labour is not in vain in the Lord.

1 Corinthians 15:58

Unto thee, O Lord, belongeth mercy: for
thou renderest to every man according to
his work.

Psalm 62:12

Jesus said, "Labour not for the meat which
perisheth, but for that meat which endureth
unto everlasting life, which the Son of man
shall give unto you."

John 6:27

Not by works of righteousness which we have done, but according to God's mercy he saved us, by the washing of regeneration, and renewing of the Holy Ghost.

Titus 3:5

Jesus said, "Come unto me, all ye that labour and are heavy laden, and I will give you rest."

Matthew 11:28

God's work is honourable and glorious: and his righteousness endureth for ever. He hath made his wonderful works to be remembered: the LORD is gracious and full of compassion.

Psalm 111:3–4

Let thy work appear unto thy servants, and
thy glory unto their children. And let the
beauty of the LORD our God be upon us: and
establish thou the work of our hands upon us;
yea, the work of our hands establish thou it.

Psalm 90:16–17

Walk worthy of the Lord unto all pleasing,
being fruitful in every good work, and
increasing in the knowledge of God;
Strengthened with all might, according to his
glorious power, unto all patience and
longsuffering with joyfulness.

Colossians 1:10–11

WORRY

Jesus said, "Take no thought for your life, what ye shall eat, or what ye shall drink; nor yet for your body, what ye shall put on. Is not the life more than meat, and the body than raiment? Behold the fowls of the air: for they sow not, neither do they reap, nor gather into barns; yet your heavenly Father feedeth them. Are ye not much better than they? Which of you by taking thought can add one cubit unto his stature? And why take ye thought for raiment? Consider the lilies of the field, how they grow; they toil not, neither do they spin: And yet I say unto you, That even Solomon in all his glory was not arrayed like one of these."

Matthew 6:25–29

Delight thyself also in the LORD; and he shall give thee the desires of thine heart.

Psalm 37:4

Where no counsel is, the people fall: but in the multitude of counsellors there is safety.

Proverbs 11:14

Cast thy burden upon the LORD, and he shall sustain thee: he shall never suffer the righteous to be moved.

Psalm 55:22

When thou liest down, thou shalt not be afraid: yea, thou shalt lie down, and thy sleep shall be sweet. Be not afraid of sudden fear, neither of the desolation of the wicked, when it cometh. For the LORD shall be thy confidence, and shall keep thy foot from being taken.

Proverbs 3:24–26

Commit thy works unto the LORD, and thy thoughts shall be established.

Proverbs 16:3

WORSHIP

Great is the LORD, and greatly to be praised:
he also is to be feared above all gods.

1 Chronicles 16:25

The LORD liveth; and blessed be my rock;
and exalted be the God of the rock of
my salvation.

2 Samuel 22:47

I will praise thee, O LORD, with my whole
heart; I will show forth all thy marvellous
works. I will be glad and rejoice in thee: I
will sing praise to thy name, O thou
most High.

Psalm 9:1–2

I will praise thee, Lord; for I am fearfully and
wonderfully made: marvellous are thy works;
and that my soul knoweth right well.

Psalm 139:14

Give unto the LORD, O ye mighty, give unto
the LORD glory and strength. Give unto the
LORD the glory due unto his name; worship
the LORD in the beauty of holiness.

Psalm 29:1–2

Jesus saith, "The hour cometh, and now is,
when the true worshippers shall worship the
Father in spirit and in truth: for the Father
seeketh such to worship him."

John 4:23

MY FAVORITE VERSES:

_____

_____

_____

_____

_____

_____

_____

_____

_____

_____

_____

_____

_____

We want to hear from you. Please send your
comments about this book to:

Inspirio, The gift group of Zondervan
5300 Patterson Ave SE
Grand Rapids, MI 49530